DON VU

FOREWORD BY DONALYN MILLER

LIFE, LITERACY, and the PURSUIT of HAPPINESS

Supporting Our Immigrant and Refugee Children Through the Power of Reading

SCHOLASTIC

For Hien and Nguyet

*For the countless tired and poor who have come before
and the huddled masses who will come after.*

Publisher/Content editor: Lois Bridges
Editorial director: Sarah Longhi
Editor-in-chief/Development editor: Raymond Coutu
Senior editor: Shelley Griffin
Production editor: Danny Miller
Designer: Maria Lilja

CONTENTS

ACKNOWLEDGMENTS

Donalyn Miller, who, even after watching my very disastrous presentation on literacy a few years ago (imagine a frozen computer, sliding microphone stand, profuse sweating), encouraged me to write a book. I am eternally grateful for her kindness and support.

I also thank the merry band of book lovers at Scholastic Book Fairs whom I have gotten to know, be inspired by, and continue to learn from these past few years. From Bill Barrett to John Schu to all of our PAB and CAB members, thank you.

A special thanks goes to Anne Wissinger and Alan Boyko for their encouragement to press on. They introduced me to Lois Bridges, whose passion, encouragement, and expertise have been invaluable in this journey. Thank you, Lois, for believing in my story and doing everything in your power to share it with the world.

Thank you to the rest of the Scholastic Professional team: Ray Coutu, Sarah Longhi, Shelley Griffin, Danny Miller, and Maria Lilja. Your skill and talent have made my first experience in publishing a blessing. You all make it look so easy!

Throughout the writing process, I've trusted my words with a small group of friends and colleagues. Thank you to Debbie V. Neighbors, Lori Oczkus, Todd Nesloney, and Jen Molino for your support. And to Terry Thompson, who was there with me from the first draft.

Thank you to the people who were there when this reading journey really took flight: Joanne Devine and my friends at PARC and the California Reading Association. And, of course, there is no book without the amazing teachers, staff, parents, and students at Barrett Ranch. You are truly the best in the universe.

Finally, a very special note of gratitude to Maria and Cate, my two loves. Thank you for your enduring love, loyalty, sacrifice, and support. This all means nothing without you.

FOREWORD

Walking around Barrett Ranch Elementary School, you can feel the positive reading culture—enticing book nooks offer students playful, peaceful spaces to curl up with books and read, and hallways and classrooms display book recommendations and other visible celebrations of reading and readers. There are books everywhere—a Little Free Library out front, abundant classroom libraries, books in the school office, and a school library. Engaging students with reading begins with ensuring continuous access to books, but it doesn't end there....

Where there are books, there are readers. Kids browse library shelves and classroom bins, talk with teachers and classmates about books, and eagerly share their book recommendations and opinions. Talking with students and teachers, it's clear that this reading community values all types of reading—graphic novels, picture books, series fiction, electronic and audio books—and every book has its reader. A supportive, inclusive reading community values all readers and their tastes. Barrett Ranch's readers know that their opinions about books and reading matter. This safety and respect feeds their confidence as readers and people.

I wish you could visit the school with me, but I am thrilled that Barrett Ranch's former principal, Don Vu, takes you inside the school's culture-building framework and the outcomes of their school's program for teachers, students, and families. Don is a wonderful storyteller, and his honest essays about himself and his family, their escape from the Vietnam days before Saigon fell, his life as an immigrant child, and his experiences and memories of reading illustrate the lasting influence of families, teachers, and books. Don is also an inclusive and responsive school leader, and credits school staff and families with driving change at the school. He stresses that any shift or initiative in a school's culture driven solely by its leaders is unsustainable. Barrett Ranch's supportive, thriving, inclusive reading community didn't pop up overnight or during one school year, and maintaining it requires constant support. Changing a reading culture schoolwide requires the effort and dedication of more than a handful of enthusiastic teachers, the school librarian, or even a literacy-minded principal like Don Vu.

How did they do it? The staff, families, and community partners at Barrett Ranch committed to long-term changes in systems and beliefs when they realized that many students were disengaged and unmotivated to read for enjoyment. They built a shared understanding of the importance of reading widely and the benefits—both intellectual and social—of developing lifelong reading habits.

Determined to change the reading culture of Barrett Ranch, they increased students' access to current, engaging books at school and home. Don and the staff reconfigured the school schedule to accommodate regular times for independent reading and read-alouds. They evaluated special education program materials and their intervention schedule to ensure that all students received opportunities to read books of their choice—with appropriate support. They expanded family engagement and literacy programs. Teachers worked to improve their practices—working in collaborative teams to support students and participating in self-directed and campus-wide professional development.

The school culture and reading instruction shifts implemented at Barrett Ranch have benefited all students, but Don and his staff were particularly concerned about meeting the literacy and community needs of immigrant and refugee children and families. Reflecting on his school experiences and the experiences of many other immigrant and refugee children, Dr. Vu and the staff sought to build a more inclusive and responsive environment at Barrett Ranch.

While Barrett Ranch has won international and national accolades for its reading program, Don emphasizes it is not a "dream school." This culture is possible for children because the adults in their lives—caregivers, parents, teachers, and community members—strive to remove obstacles that prevent many of them from developing a love for reading and reaching their literacy potential.

Above all, the teachers and families at Barrett Ranch believe that all children benefit from positive reading experiences, along with high-quality reading instruction. Kids who read widely and voluminously will learn a lot. Kids who like reading will read more. It's not magical. Even the most fragile reader benefits from a reading community that is filled with books, dedicates time for reading, encourages choice, and values the knowledge and experiences children and families bring to school.

Life, Literacy, and the Pursuit of Happiness is rich in practical strategies, thought-provoking conversation topics, student and teacher voices, and inspiration. It is possible for all children to experience reading joy and succeed on short-term measures of success like standardized tests, but Barrett Ranch and schools like it show that when we focus on engaging and supporting readers and their families, children succeed and retain an appreciation for reading. Don Vu and the Barrett Ranch community have given us a gift—a glimpse into the messy but gratifying process of reimagining what reading looks like in our schools.

—Donalyn Miller
January 2021

INTRODUCTION

*"Reading is not walking on the words;
it's grasping the soul of them."*

—PAULO FREIRE

A couple of years ago, I was in Austin, Texas, at the International Literacy Association's annual conference to receive the Exemplary Reading Program Award for my school, Barrett Ranch Elementary School in Antelope, California, one of four schools in the country to receive that prestigious award. It was a humbling experience given some of the superstars of education who were also receiving awards that day. For example, Irene Fountas and Gay Su Pinnell received a lifetime award just before we took the stage. I glanced over at Karina Almanza and Corrie Traynor—two stalwarts of our teaching staff—and whispered excitedly, "We have most of their books!" We felt a little overwhelmed and overjoyed, and reflected throughout the evening about how we got here. We traveled from a small school a few miles north of Sacramento to represent a passionate and dedicated team of educators who will go to the ends of the earth to engage kids in reading. So how did we get to this awards ceremony in the first place?

After being inspired by the work of Donalyn Miller and Steven Layne, a group of us at Barrett Ranch decided to do something about our reading culture. We noticed that our kids were doing well learning the fundamentals of reading, which says a lot about our core and intervention programs, since half of our students are classified as "emergent bilinguals," the term I use to recognize the fact that there is value in both the students' primary language, as well as their target language. Also, 70 percent of our students are considered socioeconomically disadvantaged.

However, despite the fact that our kids had a handle on reading fundamentals, we noticed that, for many of them, their progress was stagnating, and fewer students were advancing as readers. They weren't reading more than what was required because they didn't *want* to. How could they become better readers if they didn't read? We came to realize that though we were teaching our kids to read, we weren't really encouraging them to be readers. We needed to make some changes that would instill in them the joy of what it means to be a lifelong reader.

So we did what most educators do—we formed a committee: the Spark the Fire Committee (a nod to Steven Layne's *Igniting a Passion for Reading*) whose sole purpose, my colleagues and I decided, was to come up with ways to get kids and adults excited about books. Reading books. Sharing books. Talking about books. We called our effort the "Broncos Read..." campaign (our mascot is Bucky the Bronco), and gradually the entire campus participated. Teachers, students, and parents started working together to share their excitement about reading. We tried new ideas and tweaked old ways of doing things. During our journey, we learned a great deal about the impact of reading on children, adults, and the community.

About This Book

According to an old Chinese saying, "If you want to know the road ahead, ask those coming back." While I am under no delusion that I have all the answers, I wrote this book to share with you what I've learned so far in my journey. This is a professional resource designed to remind us of the power of literacy and how we can use it to make the greatest impact on all of our students, especially our immigrants and refugees. But it's also a very personal book for me. Throughout the book, in "Prelude" sections before the chapters, I weave the story of how my family and I came here as homeless Vietnamese refugees in 1975 and forged a life as new Americans. Like so many others', our story of the search for the American Dream is one of hope and resilience. Whether you serve students and families who are new to this country, my hope is that after reading this book, you will at least feel you have connected to one immigrant and his story. And with that connection between us, may we be reminded that our good work in schools and communities can not only change the lives of our immigrant and refugee students, it can also change our world.

PART I

LIFE

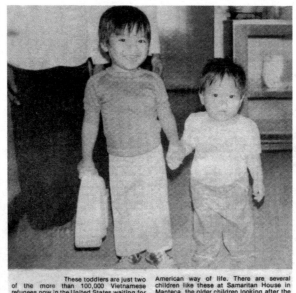

These toddlers are just two of the more than 100,000 Vietnamese refugees now in the United States waiting for someone like you to help them relocate, to help them become accustomed to the American way of life. There are several children like these at Samaritan House in Manteca, the older children looking after the younger ones.

My younger brother and I found ourselves on the front page of a local newspaper in 1975.

REFUGEES AMONG US

I HAVE NO CHILDHOOD MEMORIES OF BEING READ to at home. It's not that my parents were neglectful or absent. It's not that they didn't believe in the importance of reading to children. They just couldn't read the books.

In late April of 1975, my parents made a quick decision that most of us can't even fathom. We were living in South Vietnam, and it was almost certain that our country was going to fall to the communist North. The fighting had intensified in the capital city of Saigon, and my father, who worked as an electrician at the

U.S. Embassy, had heard whispers from the Americans that they were leaving within days. The writing was on the wall: The democratic South, without the military support of the United States, would crumble immediately. My father would be considered a traitor for working for the enemy and his punishment would have been severe. If he were lucky enough to avoid a death sentence, he would surely endure a lengthy sentence in a "re-education" camp. When the U.S.-backed president, Nguyen Van Thieu, resigned on April 21st and fled the country, the decision was made.

The very next evening, my parents hurriedly packed two bags of clothes, about $10 worth of Vietnamese currency, and a gold necklace. They knew at least the gold was worth something. They, along with my maternal and paternal grandmothers, my six-year-old cousin, my eight-month-old brother, and me (almost three years old at that time), left our house for the coastal city of Vũng Tàu, several hours away. They had planned to meet with some relatives who had connections to a shipping business owner who would charter a boat to a neighboring country, such as Malaysia or Indonesia, and seek temporary refuge there. When we arrived on the dock in the middle of the night, my parents realized that they didn't have enough money to cover the fare for all of us. Dejected, we returned home to Saigon.

The next day, my dad went to work at the embassy. One of his co-workers was shocked to see him and said, "You need to get out! It's over. We lost our country and they're flying us out." He handed my dad an official-looking document written in English and told him to make a copy of it—and add the names of all the family members who would be leaving.

That night, my dad, on a borrowed typewriter, made an almost identical copy of the certificate that would allow us to board the buses at the U.S. Embassy that would eventually take us to Tân Sơn Nhất airport. He could have waited for an official certificate, but that was a risk he was unwilling to take.

In the middle of a cold morning on April 25, 1975, we ran up a ramp into the open belly of a C-130 military plane, joined hundreds of other frightened and confused Vietnamese, and flew away from the only country we'd ever known. Saigon fell to the North a few days later on April 30th—the Americans had left and the Vietnam War was unofficially over.

There were so many questions left unanswered. How long were we going to be gone? If we did eventually return to Vietnam, would our house still be ours? Where exactly were we going? How were we going to survive in a new country? My parents were in their early twenties. They were barely old enough to legally drink. Furthermore, my younger brother and I were feverishly ill during the entire journey.

Nonetheless, our family was one of the lucky ones. For years after the war, many Vietnamese perished in the oceans on fishing boats, trying to escape their war-torn homeland. And many of those who remained behind faced years of imprisonment in "re-education" camps run by the new communist regime. America gave my family a new beginning. And for this, I am forever indebted. As it does today for many refugees and immigrants, the United States represented a beacon of hope for a brighter future.

With sudden cultural and language barriers in our new home of Manteca, California, reading aloud wasn't a thing in our house growing up. Being in survival mode didn't allow for indulging in anything but making ends meet. Given the choice of paying the electricity bill or buying a children's book, my parents chose what any parent would have chosen. And on occasions when I would bring home a book from the school library, they left the reading to us kids because our limited English skills had already surpassed their non-English skills.

For the same reason, my parents never involved themselves in my school. They were just learning not only the English language, but also American culture, and didn't feel there was a place for them—newly arrived immigrants—in my school. The schools were just beginning to respond to the recent influx of refugees from Southeast Asia; the lack of understanding and resources left many families on their own to struggle.

My parents focused on the importance of their children's education. They viewed literacy as critical for success in their new country. Being unable to read, write, and communicate in English limited their own abilities. They had traveled across the world to give their children a brighter future in a foreign land, and they were determined that those children would be as literate as any American child. Literacy meant freedom. They knew that reading was important. They just couldn't do it for us at home.

Life, Literacy, and the Pursuit of Happiness

1

THE PROMISE OF THE AMERICAN DREAM

"The American Dream belongs to all of us."

—VICE PRESIDENT KAMALA HARRIS

"Thank you for teach our son," she said.

The young mother concentrated so hard to put together that sentence and smiled in relief when she did. With confidence, she attempted a couple more words but they were unintelligible, so she gave up and turned to her son. She spoke quickly in Spanish. Roberto turned to me, avoiding eye contact, and translated, "My mom says that she is working a second job at night and can't help me with my homework, so thank you for helping me."

I turned to Roberto's mom, speaking slowly to allow the boy to translate. "You're welcome. It's my job, but Roberto is a hard worker. I will do everything I can to help your son be successful in school."

I may have sounded confident to Roberto and his mom, but the truth was this was my first parent conference as a new Teach For America teacher in the Oakland Unified School District. I was a 21-year-old kid straight out of the University of California, Berkeley, and I was in way over my head. The organization didn't give us new teachers much professional training before we stepped into the classroom, and I was overwhelmed for much of my first year. For relief, after escorting the kids to lunch, I would sneak back into my classroom and curl up under my desk for a nap to recuperate from the morning's activities. Teaching was exhausting. Because there was such a need for teachers in Oakland (like so many other urban and rural towns across America), school districts had no choice but to issue inexperienced teachers emergency credentials. It was either hire a long-term substitute for the year or a young college graduate like me. I didn't have the experience, but I did have a strong desire to make a difference.

Back in the 1990s, as it still is today, Oakland's population was a mix of recent immigrants from Southeast Asia, Mexico, and Latin America, as well as generations of Black Americans who initially moved to the West Coast for work during World War II. Most of the students at my school were from socioeconomically challenged backgrounds and many were far below proficiency academically. Teach For America was still young and had just recruited its fourth class of bright college graduates for school districts facing teacher shortages. It was a little bit like the Peace Corps, except that recruits went into the inner cities of America instead of developing countries throughout the world. My fellow teachers and I all wanted to change the world, and many of us quickly realized that changing the world is an overwhelming task. Some of my colleagues quit before their two-year commitment was up. Some, like me, stuck with Teach For America longer than anticipated.

I don't remember much of my parent conference with Roberto beyond what I shared at the start of this chapter. But I do remember looking at his mom and seeing a reflection of my own mother. How could I not? Their storylines were too similar. Leaving a home country for a better life. Struggling to assimilate into a new culture and learn a new language. Recognizing education as a door to a brighter future for your children. Feeling like an outcast in your new country. Throughout conference week, I met with other families from similar situations. Recent immigrants from Vietnam. Mexico. Cambodia. El Salvador. Even some nonimmigrant families expressed frustration that there wasn't a place for them in society. For example, Black families were frustrated because they had experienced this struggle to succeed for generations and the school system did little to help them. Some even thought that the system hurt them. Even today, I'm told, those families are feeling the same way—if Black lives matter, then they should matter in our schools.

After two and a half decades of doing this work, I wish I could say that things have gotten better. For some, things have. Some of my first students and I keep in touch, and I am happy to report that many of them are realizing the promise of the American Dream. They've attended some of the best universities in the world—Stanford, Berkeley, UCLA, Amherst, Oxford. They now work as teachers, doctors, researchers, chefs, and business owners. They are active in their communities and have their own children in schools. They continue to reinforce the importance of education for the next generation of Americans.

At a recent reunion of former students, I asked one of them, Hai, who is now a pediatrician, what she believed helped make a difference in her early years.

"I wanted more because I knew that there was more out there in this world. I knew that education was a way to get there. People like you believed in me, and I believed in myself after a while."

I wanted more because I knew that there was more out there in this world. I knew that education was a way to get there. People like you believed in me, and I believed in myself after a while.

Unfortunately, however, many of my other former students have never escaped the margins of American society. Some never finished high school. Some fell victim to gangs. Some were incarcerated. They are the next generation that struggles to realize the ever-elusive promise of America—and unfortunately, a disproportionate number come from communities of color. It's apparent just by turning on the television and watching the news, reading the newspaper, or just paying attention in our schools and communities. When we examine the persistent opportunity gap, the disparities in graduation rates, and the differences in how children are disciplined based on color first, behavior second, it becomes crystal clear that the American Dream is not as reachable for some as it is for others.

2

THE WORK BEFORE US

*"Until we reach equality in education,
we can't reach equality in the larger society."*

—JUSTICE SONIA SOTOMAYOR

Literacy is freedom. Well, it is for some. Around the same time Dr. Rudine Sims Bishop made popular the metaphor of "windows, mirrors, and sliding glass doors" to describe children's literature in the 1990s, we educators were in the midst of the "multicultural" movement in Oakland schools. What Dr. Bishop meant was that books and stories can act as windows in which children see a world outside of their own, or mirrors in which they see a reflection of themselves in the world. They can act as sliding glass doors by inviting children to pass through them into other worlds (Bishop, 1990). In Oakland, it was essential for the curriculum to represent children's cultures, especially in books and stories, because many of our students were not from the American mainstream. The only problem: 30 years ago, there were very few books and stories being published that could serve as mirrors for kids of color. I remember back then being thrilled to find a Vietnamese folktale or a picture book about Rosa Parks to share with my students.

And the problem has not gone away. Today, access to books that capture the experiences of people outside the American mainstream remains limited.

According to the Cooperative Children's Book Center, only 27 percent of all children's books published contained Black, First Nations, Asian American, Pacific Islander, or Latinx main characters (CCBD, 2020); the other 73 percent featured main characters who were white, animals, or objects.

Taking a glass-half-full approach, the same group's study four years earlier showed that only 13.5 percent of all children's books published featured underrepresented characters. And taking another sip from the glass, nonprofit organizations, such as We Need Diverse Books, are emerging and promoting more inclusive books and working with publishers to support the authors and illustrators who create them. Their mission is clear—putting more books featuring diverse characters into the hands of all children. And it's working. We are seeing more authors from different backgrounds—such as Angie Thomas, Erika Sanchez, and Minh Lê—writing stories for children who yearn to see themselves in books. While there has been much progress in the last few years, there is still much work to do.

And the problem is not just about a lack of access to books with diverse characters. It's about a lack of access to books, period. Kids who live in low-income communities can have up to 4,000 times fewer books available to them than those who live in high-income communities (Neuman & Celano, 2001; Neuman & Celano, 2012). Furthermore, poorer students tend to have fewer books at home and no bookstores or libraries nearby. The disparity is so common nowadays that there's a term for the reality of poorer students: book deserts.

Even when we find books for them, our poorer students and immigrant and refugee students are too often still at a disadvantage. Some don't have opportunities to read at home or with an adult who can read to and with them. Some don't have opportunities to read during their holiday breaks or summer vacation and, as such, experience a slide in their reading proficiency upon returning to school. Some don't have opportunities to talk with family members about what they are reading or should be reading. Some don't have reading role models to inspire them to make books an integral part of their lives. This happens for many possible reasons, ranging from the limited English proficiency of adults in the house to adults working several jobs to make ends meet and not having as many opportunities to read with younger children. While those challenges don't automatically doom a child to a life without literacy, they do put children at risk of never fully experiencing the joy and benefits of reading—and to view a world beyond their own through the window of a book, or to relate to a character so deeply, they feel they're staring at themselves in a mirror.

If literacy is freedom, then every child in America should have equal access to it.

If literacy is freedom, then every child in America should have equal access to it. Unfortunately, not every child does. Educators have a hand in this.

In his research, Richard Allington describes the teaching of exemplary elementary teachers, based on thousands of hours of observation and interviews conducted by him and his team (Allington, 2002). While subsequent studies have been conducted by Allington and other reading researchers, his initial findings have withstood the test of time.

Time: Exemplary teachers allocated significantly more time for kids to read and write throughout the day than their counterparts.

Texts: Exemplary teachers provided a rich supply of reading materials, which students read at a high level of accuracy, fluency, and comprehension.

Teach: Exemplary teachers routinely offered direct instruction of effective reading strategies, and modeled thinking and reading skills for students.

Talk: Exemplary teachers encouraged, modeled, and supported purposeful talk throughout the day.

Tasks: Exemplary teachers provided students with substantive, meaningful work that engaged and challenged them. Often students had a choice in tasks they were assigned.

Test: Exemplary teachers based their evaluations more on students' effort and improvement than on their achievement.

Allington noticed, too, that most of the teachers he studied did not always align their work with school or district curricular frameworks. For instance, at times, they replaced components of the prescribed curriculum with independent reading. Or they'd use their own funds to supplement their classroom libraries so their students would have a wide choice of reading materials. In other words, the teachers did their extraordinary work *in spite of* the school and district's less effective structures and policies. Allington says, "It really seems unfortunate that so many of the exemplary teachers we studied were forced to teach against the organizational grain. These teachers had to reject school and district plans that put the same reader, trade book, textbook, or workbook on every child's desk. They had to reject scripted lessons, pacing schedules, and grading schemes that presented a one-size-fits-all model for instruction" (Allington, 2002).

Allington challenges school administrators to examine their practices by asking themselves how they can help create systems in schools and/or districts that foster and support truly effective reading instruction. If we know what exemplary teaching looks like, doesn't it make sense to create schools that support it? Allington summarizes with a call to action: "Schools and school districts must take more responsibility for providing instructional and curricular support so that exemplary teaching becomes more common and requires far less effort. Good teaching should not have to work against the organizational grain" (Allington, 2002).

If we know what exemplary teaching looks like, doesn't it make sense to create schools that support it?

Yes, let's create conditions for a culture of literacy in our schools so teachers don't have to work against what they're being told to do to engage kids. But let's also pay special attention to the lives of our immigrants and refugees, our students who are perpetually trapped in an opportunity gap, and our students who struggle to find a place in the American mainstream. How do we create a culture of literacy for them so they can thrive? How do we train our teaching staff, change our practices, and reorganize to support and nurture a lifelong love of literacy for all? And how can we use literacy to promote a more just, equitable, and respectful society? By thinking deeply about those questions, we will not only lift up the disenfranchised, but all who walk through our school and classroom doors.

3

WHY CAN'T WE ALL HAVE THIS?

"Where there is no vision, there is no hope."

—GEORGE WASHINGTON CARVER

Imagine for a moment that you are visiting a school you've never visited before. As you approach the campus, you notice a few things: Kids from all walks of life are walking with books in their hands; some are even reading those books as they navigate their way to class. As you enter the campus, you see kids browsing a Little Free Library set up outside, searching for the next book to read. You see on the school marquee several events scheduled for the month: a family literacy night, an author visit, and a book fair. You go to the office to check in.

The office staff greets you warmly. You look around and notice that the posters and signs are welcoming, translated into various languages for families that are new to the country. You also notice a poster advertising after-school language lessons, suggesting that learning a new language is not reserved for only non-English speakers. You get a sense that everyone here sees the world as a big place, and that culture and language are to be respected and valued.

The principal invites you into her office, which looks more like a reading lounge than a traditional administrator's space. The chairs look more conducive to reading than discipline. Books are everywhere; the ones on display represent not only the students in the school, but also the world at large. There are classics and new offerings that you would find in the recently released section at the local bookstore. You want to peruse the collection, but you are invited to tour the campus.

During your tour, you see more kids reading— independently, with friends, and in groups. They look like they come from all over the world, but they are not segregated by race or ethnicity. They are grouped by common interests and passions. Those who are not reading are listening to someone else read, or they are talking to someone about what they've read. They laugh and joke. They are debating observations and issues, and having critical conversations about the world. You are amazed as you pass by all the little nooks and crannies throughout the school where kids can just sit down with a book and read.

As in the principal's office, books are everywhere. Every classroom has an extensive library with the most exciting and engaging books available. As you look at the daily schedules on classroom whiteboards, you notice that teachers have included times for kids to read independently, as well as times to conference with them. In other words, time is reserved for reading and for talking about what kids are reading. Nothing feels rushed, and you get a strong sense that kids are learning that reading should rarely be rushed.

Students are at every level of reading proficiency. Those who are just learning English are being taught foundational skills, without sacrificing authentic reading opportunities. They are using books as windows into the American culture that they are now immersed in. The more advanced readers are working on projects that allow them to reflect on and explore their interests and passions in the real world. No matter where they are in their reading life, the students seem supported and engaged.

Your tour ends in the school library. By the number of students congregating in this space, you can tell right away that the library is a cool place to be. The librarian shows you to the most popular books and, of course, you see more kids reading. The culture of literacy in this school is palpable. You can feel it like you can feel the warm sun on a summer day. It is clear that joyful reading is a priority for this community. You can also feel a sense of pride in all students—a sense that they know they belong at this school. The stories they read and the stories they tell, both orally and in writing, have value and contribute to the life of the community.

The culture of literacy in this school is palpable. You can feel it like you can feel the warm sun on a summer day. It is clear that joyful reading is a priority for this community.

And you ask yourself, "Why can't all schools be like this?"

That is not only a good question, it is a critical question. Many people would say that this "dream school" is just that—a fantasy that can't exist universally. They might argue that there's no way to get funding. They might argue that, with all the educational

Life, Literacy, and the Pursuit of Happiness

mandates imposed on teachers and administrators, there isn't enough time in the day for students to engage so deeply in reading. They might argue that, even if we found the time, only a handful of kids would engage in books and literacy to that extent. They might argue that this type of multicultural kumbaya is not possible given the reality of our racially divided society.

If we can't imagine the possibilities, then there's no way of ever getting there.

To those people, I argue that this vision of schools is exactly what we need— and that it is achievable. If we can't imagine the possibilities, then there's no way of ever getting there. If literacy is freedom, let's envision what it could look like for us and all our students.

4

THE CONDITIONS FOR A CULTURE OF LITERACY FOR ALL

"If you attempt to implement reforms but fail to engage the culture of a school, nothing will change."

—SEYMOUR SARASON

While some schools have been successful in creating and sustaining a culture similar to the one described in Chapter 3, all too many haven't. Many literacy efforts in schools involve particular programs or strategies, and they are often kept afloat by the work and will of strong literacy leaders. However, when things shift, as they always do in education, the sustainability of those efforts are determined mostly by the culture that is built around them. When programs, strategies, and even school leaders come and go, is the school's culture strong enough to leave no doubt of its commitment to literacy and justice for all? Will the culture continue to support the continuing efforts to make all kids lifelong readers and thinkers? Organizational researcher Peter

Drucker once said, "Culture eats strategy for breakfast." While his research focused primarily on business, his assertion can easily be applied to education. Culture is key to everything, and if we want to have a school like the one described in Chapter 3, we must explore the conditions of culture closely.

The culture of an organization is the set of shared values, practices, customs, and traditions that help define it. Culture is what makes any organization unique, and individuals need to learn how to behave within it. To illustrate, let's take a closer look at an institution we're all a part of: the United States of America. What makes our country's culture unique? To answer that question, ask yourself this: "What's most important to Americans?" If you look up the top 10 things Americans search for on the Internet, your search results will likely show topics that range from celebrities to natural disasters to national or local news. Of course, this is no solid scientific study, but it does give us insight into what we value as a nation.

What results might you expect to find if you could do a similar search on your campus or in your district? What would pop up as universally important to your stakeholders? Every school has a culture that makes it unique. It's the result of the shared values, goals, and practices of the staff, students, parents, and community. The culture of the school is important because, as Peter Drucker would attest, everything that is done in a school is impacted by its culture. Some of us are lucky enough to work in schools and districts where the culture is generally positive and everyone is working

The Barrett Ranch staff posing with their favorite books

together toward common goals. Everyone shares the values, goals, and practices, and everyone is supported in his or her work.

Unfortunately, in some schools and districts, the opposite is true. No one is collaborating and, instead, everyone is working independently, with little or no support. Teachers are tired and burned out. There is no sense of community or trust, and there is often talk about "us versus them." Imagine if a staff member from this type of school came up with the idea to engage all kids in reading books on a schoolwide level. What do you think are the chances of this idea being accepted? I would guess slim to none. No matter how great or innovative an idea or strategy is, the culture of an organization often determines its success.

Before some of you get discouraged and close this book because you indeed work in a school with a negative culture, there is good news. Culture is organic and, therefore, dynamic. Values, goals, and practices shift. What is important today may not be important tomorrow. In the same vein, values, goals, and practices being neglected today can be prioritized tomorrow, and help eventually redefine a culture. While it requires much work to change and build the culture of any school, it is definitely not impossible.

What if we expand and refine Allington's ideas of exemplary reading instruction, which I described in Chapter 2, to work on an organizational level in schools? That's what Allington asks us to do anyway—change the organizational grain so that exemplary teaching can thrive (Allington, 2002).

A deeper exploration will show that there are six conditions that help create a culture of literacy for all, where excitement about reading takes hold and flourishes in schools and districts: *Commitment*, *Clock*, *Collection*, *Conversation*, *Connection*, and *Celebration*. In the following chapters, I will examine those conditions in depth, in the context of research, best practices, and implementation of strategies and ideas.

For now, let's take the discussion beyond building a thriving culture of literacy and ask ourselves, "Why do we want our kids to become lifelong readers?" The answer is simple. We want every one of our students to fulfill his or her potential and promise. For that to happen, we need to create and sustain not just a culture of literacy, but a culture of literacy that supports social justice, equity, and respect for oneself and others. How can we include every member of our school community? How can we use literacy to acknowledge, elevate, and celebrate students and families who are traditionally left outside the margins of society? And how can we use literacy to make our schools, our communities, and the world better places for all? When we look at our jobs as educators in that light, the responsibility for the future looms larger than ever. We've become more than teachers, librarians, and administrators. We're not just in it for the day or even the school year, we are in it for a lifetime. We've become the keepers of the promise and hope for a brighter future.

PART II

LITERACY

From my dad's wallet, one of only two photos of myself as a child (on the left) in Vietnam. The rest were lost in the chaotic aftermath of war.

IN THE UNLIKELY EVENT OF A SUDDEN LOSS OF CABIN PRESSURE

THE C-130 IS CONSIDERED THE SWISS ARMY KNIFE of military planes. It's been used in war to drop bombs, carry equipment, deploy troops, launch drones, and much more. One reason for its versatility is its fuselage—the main body of the plane. At approximately 41 feet long, 9 feet high, and 10 feet wide, it's huge. As such, it can carry 10,000-pound bombs, which can be released during flight through a rear hatch. While it is a machine used primarily for destruction in war, the C-130 became a symbol of salvation for many Vietnamese in the final days of the Vietnam War.

On the morning of my family's departure from Vietnam, from our home, my parents had moments of second thoughts. As we boarded the bus to Tân Sơn Nhất Airport, my mom told my eager dad that she didn't want to leave because my younger brother and I were sick. She suggested going back home and waiting until our fevers subsided. At least, the journey would be more tolerable, she thought. (She and my father could not have known that every day leading up to the final evacuation of the American Embassy would bring more chaos and confusion.) Something in the back of my parents' minds told them to continue forward.

Both of my grandmothers were also hesitant to go, as they would be leaving many of their other children and grandchildren behind. My paternal grandmother would also be leaving her husband behind— he had been working on a farm in a town near the coast of Vietnam and could not make it back to Saigon in time. But they boarded the plane nonetheless, comforted by the thought that this was possibly a temporary evacuation and that they would return home when the dust settled. Little did they know that day would be their last in Vietnam.

The C-130 was designed to carry as many as 90 paratroopers for deployment into battle. But the chaos of the Vietnam War made policies, regulations, maximum capacity, and operational limits moot. It was reported that, in one evacuation flight from Saigon, 452 Vietnamese refugees disembarked from the belly of one C-130 after it had safely landed in a Thai Air Force base. While I'm not sure if our plane's capacity came close to that number, I have been told that it was packed like a can of sardines, everyone sitting on the fuselage floor.

We landed on the tiny island of Guam by way of the Philippines, as a part of a resettlement program called Operation New Life. Along with 110,000 other Vietnamese refugees, my family members and I existed in purgatory, waiting in a tent city near the coast of Guam, oblivious to where we were off to next. A week later, we were informed that we would be leaving the next day for our final destination—Camp Pendleton. San Diego, California. The United States of America.

My father doesn't remember much about the flight across the Pacific Ocean from Guam to San Diego. He told me, with a smile, that it was much more comfortable than the initial flight in the C-130. It was the first time my family had been in a plane designed for civilian travel, and he remembered the warning over the intercom: Passengers were given strict instructions to secure their own mask before helping others—including their children—in the unlikely event of a sudden loss of cabin pressure. That stuck with him because his first instinct was always to help his wife and children. And it made sense. After all, how could he help anyone if he was passed out on the cabin floor? The idea was simple. Make sure that you take care of yourself first so that you can take care of the others around you.

The Conditions for a Culture of Literacy for All

As I mentioned in Chapter 4, there are six conditions that help create a culture of literacy for all, where excitement about reading takes hold and flourishes in schools and districts:

- Commitment
- Clock
- Collection
- Conversation
- Connection
- Celebration

In the remainder of this book, I devote a chapter to each of those conditions to help you understand how and why it is vital to school and student success.

5

COMMITMENT

"That's at the core of equity: understanding who your kids are and how to meet their needs. You are still focused on outcomes, but the path to get there may not be the same for each one."

—PEDRO NOGUERA

Just like the pre-flight instructions that remind you to secure your oxygen mask first before you help others, educators need to remember to take care of themselves first so that they can take care of their students and families. Commitment is the first condition to creating a culture of literacy for all. I start with commitment because it acknowledges the fact that we must prioritize educators and practice self-care and personal growth. If your goal is to build and sustain a school environment that encourages a lifelong love of literacy in all children, then adults, too, must have a love of literacy. Indeed, if we want to educate and raise a generation of open-minded, understanding, respectful, and empathetic citizens of the world, then we need to make sure the educators in our schools embrace those traits. How do we create an environment that will foster those traits in our teachers and administrators? We can only expect our staffs to be able to best serve immigrant and refugee students and families when they are a part of a school culture that prioritizes using the power of literacy to lift up the lives of all students.

I realize that doing that is easier said than done. After all, educators come from all walks of life, cultures, socioeconomic groups, and religious and political affiliations. We can't expect them to walk onto the school campus and leave behind everything they feel and believe at home. There will be biases, blind spots, and differences of opinion. We all have them. And they can have a negative impact on our students. So when we commit to creating a culture of literacy for all, it's important to identify and examine our own individual perspectives that could impact our work with kids. This is the first step of this condition—a commitment to taking care of ourselves and a commitment to personal growth—so we can take care of those we serve.

Let me be clear about what commitment in an organization looks like, starting by explaining the difference between a group of committed people and a group of compliant people. In his seminal work, *The Fifth Discipline*, researcher Peter Senge (2006) describes the "compliant" employee in an organization as one who is a "good soldier" and will do what is expected of him or her. On the other hand, a "committed" employee is someone who will go above and beyond to realize the vision of the organization. A committed employee views that vision as his or her personal vision, and accepts responsibility for seeing it to fruition. Senge writes, "A group of people truly committed to a common vision is an awesome force." In fact, he identifies commitment to a shared vision as a key discipline in successful organizations.

For those of us who work in schools, the importance of commitment is no different. However, instead of focusing on the bottom line or product development, we focus on the success of our students. When building a culture of literacy for all, everyone has an important role to play. As Peter Senge discovered, commitment doesn't happen if individuals don't personalize the group vision. The question for us is, "What is the group vision and how do we establish it?"

A committed team with a shared vision can move mountains.

Commitment to a Common Vision of Literacy

What role does literacy play in your school, and how does the staff see literacy benefiting the students? I hope it plays a huge role. After all, students need to be able to read, write, and communicate in order to be successful in school and life. However, for that to happen, we need to reflect upon how important literacy is in our own lives. Your initial conversations as a staff will not only be critical in clarifying the mission and outlining the work to be done, but also in creating a sense of understanding and belonging among all participants.

When people share their stories, they connect, find common ground, and ultimately find strength in one another's company.

Fifth-grade teacher Karina Almanza shared with her team the reason literacy is so important to her. Education was not available to her grandparents, who were farm laborers from Mexico. As they settled in California, they stressed the importance of literacy and education to their children. The idea of education as a key to prosperity filtered down to their grandchildren. Karina reflects, "For my family, we had to fight to become educated. Literacy was a gift. It was important for me to share that history, as well as hear the histories of my colleagues, to understand where we all come from." When people share their stories, they connect, find common ground, and ultimately find strength in one another's company. Encouraging that kind of sharing is vital as you dig deeper into the work.

It's important to have individual reflections as well as group conversations to establish a common vision of your hope for all students and your role in helping them realize the American Dream through the power of literacy.

Explore Your Own Literate Life

Use these reflection questions as starting points for discussions with your team as you work together to find a common vision for literacy in your school. You may start by organizing staff members into small groups and then share out to the whole group. Be sure to record thoughts and ideas for future reference.

1. What are your favorite books, authors, and/or genres?

2. On a scale of 1 to 10, how would you rate your enthusiasm for reading and writing? Why do you rate yourself this way?

3. What impact has literacy had in your life so far?

At Mary Williams Elementary School in Dumfries, Virginia, principal Lynmara Colón and her staff decided to focus on literacy as a part of their school improvement plan in 2015. They worked together to craft a school vision statement that focused on literacy access for all, as they felt that not all students had that access. Emergent bilinguals weren't as engaged or challenged as their English-proficient peers. They rarely had opportunities to engage with meaningful stories and other texts, and instead were fed a steady diet of textbooks and worksheets. Principal Colón and the team kept literacy at the forefront, focusing their social media on literacy-related news and events, expanding their libraries, and constantly revisiting their vision with kids, parents, and one another. Their vision drove their work. When they found themselves veering off the path, they came back to the vision statement and recalibrated. Teachers committed to changing their practices as necessary, providing more opportunities for students to read authentic texts instead of textbooks. It wasn't easy, but their work paid off. Mary Williams went from a "School of Improvement" designation to a "School of Excellence" designation in only two years.

Commitment to Understanding the American Dream

As you embark on your journey to build a rich culture of literacy for all, I urge you to explore what the American Dream means to the educators who have been charged to guide students toward its promise. Some staff members might happily say that they are living the American Dream now—their lives are better than their parents'. They are financially stable or even thriving, their children are benefitting from an excellent education, and they are successful in their professional and personal lives. For them, the American Dream is real and they can appreciate the opportunities that have been made available to them.

Focusing on the American Dream forces us to think about the long-term effects of our work—what do we ultimately want for our students and society?

But for others, the American Dream may seem like a myth. They might be working multiple jobs and living paycheck to paycheck. They may be concerned about what the future holds for their children as they ask themselves how the next generation will deal with financial instability, social inequities, and racism. For them, the American Dream is just that—a dream that has yet to be realized.

Focusing on the American Dream forces us to think about the long-term effects of our work—what do we ultimately want for our students and society? It also forces us to think about those who are living in the margins of society—those who face more obstacles and challenges as they strive to realize this dream. It also requires us to try to understand what the American Dream means for our students and their families. Whether you are a white middle-class woman or a gay Chinese American man, it's important to articulate what it means to be an American and what it means to live in a democratic society.

Reflecting on the American Dream

Use these reflection questions as starting points for discussions with your team as you work together to transform your school. You may start by organizing staff members into small groups and then share out to the whole group.

1. What does the American Dream mean to you? In examining your own history, are you living it, have you lived it, or have you never experienced it?

2. What role did literacy play for you in realizing or not realizing the American Dream?

3. What do you believe the American Dream means to your students? What do you think it mean to refugees, immigrants, and students of color?

4. What are the obstacles that keep your students from realizing the American Dream? What could you do to help remove those obstacles?

5. How do you respond to students and families who don't believe the American Dream is possible for them?

Parents can also play an important role in shaping a vision of the American Dream. In *Powerful Partnerships: A Teacher's Guide to Engaging Families for Student Success* (2017), Dr. Karen Mapp, Ilene Carver, and Jessica Lander recommend that at the beginning of the year, schools invite parents to write a "Hopes and Dreams" letter addressed to their children, in any language, including their home language. For parents who prefer to share their thoughts verbally, teachers transcribe them. The letters, along with family photos, are displayed on

the classroom walls for the remainder of the year. Co-author and first-grade teacher Ilene Carver states, "Our children need to know that our goals and expectations for them this year are deeply rooted in the hopes, dreams, and expectations of their families; that home and school are not two separate worlds." Not only do these letters serve as powerful reminders to students of their families' hopes and dreams for them, but they also provide educators with powerful insights into what the American Dream means to the families they serve.

Commitment to Examining Ourselves

There is a danger in living in a divided society. We spend more time interacting with people who look like us and think like us, and less time with people who don't. As such, our perception of the world becomes skewed and may impact our work in schools. According to a recent U.S. Department of Education survey (2020), 79 percent of all public-school teachers in America are white, 9 percent are Hispanic, 7 percent are Black, and 2 percent are Asian American. This demographic does not reflect the student population in America—where white students are actually the minority. When we keep this in mind, we realize that it is very likely that our immigrant and refugee students will be educated by teachers who will not look like them and not have similar backgrounds and experiences as them. In every case, it is important to us educators to examine our biases and be committed to exploring perspectives other than our own.

The Pleasanton Unified School District, in a suburb near San Francisco, is annually ranked one of the top districts in California. It is also a great example of how changing demographics can cause tension when schools aren't prepared for that change. Historically made up of white middle-class families, Pleasanton has seen a sudden influx of Asian and South Asian families in the past few years, due to its proximity to Silicon Valley, as well as its reputation for high-performing schools. Asian and South Asian American students now make up almost 40 percent of the total enrollment, and white students have become the minority. The teaching staff, with a high average salary compared to other parts of the country, is relatively stable, and 94 percent of the teachers have three or more years of experience.

Initially, some teachers were concerned because parent involvement had declined significantly; families were not as engaged in the schools as they were before the new students arrived. Many of them didn't volunteer in classrooms, participate in fundraising, or attend school events. As such, it wasn't uncommon to hear in the teachers' lounge grumblings such as, "I don't get any classroom support anymore," and "The families and kids have changed so much." Instead of looking for ways to engage new families, teachers continued to complain that these families were not doing their part in helping schools improve.

It was not until a committee of teachers looked at the situation from a community perspective that they came to understand that cultural differences were at play. They realized that the Asian and South Asian communities were not comfortable crossing into what they considered the schools' roles in educating their children. They learned about cultural and language barriers that kept parents from volunteering in schools. It was a blind spot, and the teachers began to work together to reach out to those communities to find a place for them in their schools.

We don't create blind spots consciously, and no blame for them needs to be assigned. But we all have them.

According to a recent longitudinal study from the University of Oregon and the Leibniz Institute for Research and Information in Education (Umansky & Dumont, 2019), the "English learner" classification has a "direct and negative effect on teachers' perceptions of students' academic skills." Findings indicate that teachers had lower perceptions of the academic skills and knowledge of students who were classified as "English learners," regardless of the grade or subject they taught. While this study does not explore the impact of those perceptions on student achievement, it is clear that teacher bias—no matter how dedicated the staff—is a real issue in schools.

We don't create blind spots consciously, and no blame for them needs to be assigned. But we all have them.

As I stated earlier, no blame for blind spots needs to be assigned. When learning to drive a car, we accept the fact that the driver's side mirror has blind spots. It's only when you ignore those blind spots and wind up hitting another car that fault can be assigned. In the same way, when we ignore our blind spots related to our students, their families, and their backgrounds, we shoulder the blame. How do we expect to raise the next generation of open-minded readers and thinkers if we don't do everything in our power to minimize those blind spots for ourselves?

So where do we start? The first step is to identify and acknowledge our blind spots. Teachers in the Pleasanton Unified School District realized that they were not taking the cultural differences of the Asian and South Asian communities into consideration when planning school-family partnerships. Once they identified that blind spot, they were able to rethink their strategies.

In the same light, would knowing that the "English learner" classification has a negative effect on teachers' perceptions of students' academic skills be helpful to those educators working with immigrants and refugees? Conscientious teachers take the time to reflect on and be cognizant of their work with emergent bilinguals. It's not just a matter of being willing to change your approach, it's a matter of lacking the knowledge of, experience with, or exposure to a particular group of people to see the issues.

PURSUIT OF COMMITMENT

Examine Your Possible Blind Spots

Teacher and author Chad Everett says, "If our shelves are diverse but our lives are not, we have missed the mark" (2017). The point of reading and sharing diverse stories is to open our lives to the perspectives of others. So, how diverse is your life? Here are some questions you can ask yourself to identify and acknowledge any potential blind spots in your perspectives.

1. Check your social media network. How many friends do you have who are of a different race or ethnicity from yours?

2. Check your real-life social network. Who do you spend time with socially? Is it a homogeneous or heterogeneous group? Does your network include people from all walks of life?

3. How often do you engage with people from cultures and socioeconomic backgrounds other than your own? And people who hold beliefs and live lifestyles other than your own?

4. Are you exposed to a variety of opinions and perspectives through different types of media (books, radio, newspapers, online sources, etc.)?

Remember that these questions are the beginning of the conversation with the intention to lead you to more reflection and discovery. If you do find yourself living in a homogeneous bubble, acknowledge it and take steps to expand it. Not only will it equip you to help your students become future global citizens, but your life will be enriched with new ideas, interests, and friends.

What You and Your Colleagues Can Do to Expand Your Bubble

You can read anti-racist books and attend equity conferences, but if you don't connect with real people and cultures that are different from yours, you have much more work to do. What are things you can do to expand your bubble to include more diversity in your life?

Art

Visit an Asian or African art museum in a city near you, if possible. When we explore the art and culture of a people, we learn about their histories as well as their hopes for the future.

Some museums offer exhibits and programming that cut across cultures. A few years ago, for example, I visited the Museum of Tolerance in Los Angeles, California, with my district's leadership team, and it helped us to focus our discussions of bias, prejudice, and tolerance. After being immersed in conversations from historical issues of injustice (e.g., the Holocaust) to current issues (e.g., LGBTQIA discrimination), we came back to our district with a renewed commitment to pay attention to those issues in our schools and communities.

Bún Riêu—a savory tomato-based noodle soup with crab, egg, and tofu

Food

The next one's easy. Eat. Try different foods. For example, at a Vietnamese restaurant, order something that you've never had before. (I recommend the bún riêu—a savory tomato-based noodle soup with crab, egg, and tofu.) The chef and travel writer Anthony Bourdain once said, "If I'm an advocate for anything, it is to move. Across the ocean, or simply across the river. Walk in someone else's shoes or at least eat their food. It's a plus for everybody." Not only will you get to experience a different culture firsthand, you may even find a new favorite dish.

Culture

Have you read a good book or watched a good movie lately? When we read an international book or watch a foreign film, we learn about different viewpoints, explore different societies and settings, and meet characters from different backgrounds and circumstances. Isn't that the point? To open ourselves to perspectives that can help us understand the world (and our students) a little better.

I'm a big fan of YouTube and using educational videos to help kids build background knowledge and learn about different content-area topics. The same goes for adults. We can learn so much about different people, lifestyles, and cultures just by watching televised and online documentaries and travel videos. With these virtual experiences, our perspectives broaden and our bubble expands. Educational researcher Robert Marzano (2004) suggests that virtual experiences can build background knowledge and contribute to our general knowledge of the world.

If your schedule and budget allow, pack your bags and visit a foreign land. I don't mean go to a tropical resort and hang out by the pool for a week, drinking margaritas. I mean immerse yourself in a new culture. Meet the people, eat the food, try to negotiate the daily realities of the culture, and learn a bit of the language. Experience how disorienting, frustrating, and scary it can be for an outsider, as well as exciting and edifying. Immersing yourself in another culture will give you a sense of what it's like for your students and families who are experiencing the same thing in your school.

Street vendor in Hanoi

What You Can Do to Connect With People Who Are Different From You

Now for the harder part: making social connections with people who are different from you. Heck, it's hard enough to make connections with people who are similar to you, so I tip my hat to all who give it a try. Where do you start? First, you assume positive intentions of people around you. Second, you listen and learn. The workplace may be a good place to start because you will already have something in common—your jobs. Just a reminder, if you're a person of color, this applies to you, too.

While you won't initially talk about bias and prejudice, these topics may eventually come up once you've built a strong enough connection (over days, weeks, months, or years, depending on many factors), especially if you are talking about diversity issues at school. Have your colleagues of color experienced bias, prejudice, or racism? If they have, in what ways has it impacted them in their professional lives? Try to just listen with an understanding ear. It's okay to ask questions. If you're a person of color and are trying to connect with white colleagues, ask how they view bias, prejudice, and racism in society and schools. It may take a while to establish trust but, over time, you will. Once you build that bridge, the conversations you have about how to make your school and district a safe place for all people will be deeper and more meaningful.

What does the commitment to examine ourselves and our blind spots have to do with building a culture of literacy for all? If we want literacy to open the world to our students, to give them voice and enable them to see and embrace the perspectives of others, we need to be as equipped as possible to help them get there. That won't happen if we, their teachers, have blind spots that prevent us from seeing the world through the eyes of others.

Commitment to Understanding Our Students and Families

My predecessor, Jim Ferguson, was the principal who opened Barrett Ranch Elementary School in 2006. The school is located in a diverse area of the district—more than half of the families speak a language other than English at home. It was and still is a mix of recent immigrants from Russia, Ukraine, Mexico, and Latin America, as well as families who have lived in the area for generations. Because Barrett Ranch was a new school in 2006, Jim recruited many of the teachers with the promise that it was a completely different type of school. Many of those teachers had already had experience working in schools that were made up of primarily white middle-class families. Barrett Ranch was going to be the first Title I school for most of the teachers, and they were going to have to overcome not only issues related to language and culture, but also issues of poverty. He recruited the best teachers he could find. Jim recalls, "I knew that many of them were in for a culture shock. It wasn't just a shock to us as I'm sure it was a shock to the families to be thrown into a brand-new school with a bunch of strangers."

Jim decided to do something that teachers still talk about to this day. He held a staff meeting on a school bus. As they went through their agenda, the driver took the teachers through the neighborhoods where their students lived. They stopped at the apartment buildings. They checked out the convenience stores and local shops. They went into areas where kids were playing soccer in the streets. The kids and parents were surprised and delighted to see their new principal and teachers. Jim knew that this was the first step in the teachers truly understanding the community they served. He knew that, as a staff, they needed to commit to expanding their bubble and commit to understanding deeply their students and families.

If we truly want to build a culture of literacy for all, we need to commit to knowing our students.... We need to know their individual stories.

If we truly want to build a culture of literacy for all, we need to commit to knowing our students beyond the demographic data that can be found on any district website. We need to know their individual stories. Under what circumstances did they come to America? What are their challenges as new Americans in the community and in your school? What is the history of their community? What socioeconomic factors are impacting its members?

There are many ways for you to get to know your students and their community on a wide scale. For example, for the last several years in the spring, my former school partnered with neighboring schools to host a World Fair event. Our vision was to highlight and celebrate all the cultures in our schools. Families volunteered to run booths in which they shared cultural artifacts and food samples. From Russia to Mexico, nearly 30 countries were represented every year.

(top) Student performances at the Antelope Community World Fair were special.

(bottom) Enjoying the Russian booth at the World Fair.

Every student "traveler" was given a booklet for the event, a passport to be stamped as they visited the different countries. Throughout the evening, the main stage may have featured performances from a student *baile folklórico* dance group or a Ukrainian *bandura* quartet. The World Fair was a wonderful community event that not only sent a message to our families that they were valued, but also provided staff members the opportunity to interact with the families on a cultural level. Even in schools with little diversity, World Fairs can be opportunities for staff and families to study and explore other cultures.

On your own time, you can shop at the businesses in your students' neighborhoods, go to the hair salon or barbershop, eat at the restaurants. You can get your groceries at the local supermarket. Even if you don't see any of your students or their families in the neighborhood, you'll gain a better understanding of who they are by experiencing a little of their world outside of school. And if by chance you do meet some of your students and their families, you will start to build a connection and trust that will only add value to the work you do in school.

Every day on campus is an opportunity to learn more about your students and their families. Take the time to talk to the families when they visit the campus. Ask questions beyond those related to academics: "How's Grandma doing after surgery?" "How was your trip to Honduras?" A little interest goes a long way, and soon you will feel a deeper connection to your students and their families.

Commitment to Redefining Our Schools

A few years ago in a former school district of mine, my colleagues and I started the process of taking on a new social studies curriculum. An adoption committee was formed to brainstorm ideas on the most important aspects of a social studies curriculum. The committee was dedicated, passionate, and intelligent. It reflected the district's 350 teachers—mainly white women. In fact, there were no teachers or administrators of color on it. In a district with over 50 different languages and cultures represented, one would expect a call for a multicultural curriculum. But, unbelievably, the word "multicultural" never came up. For a social studies curriculum. While this is only one example of a blind spot, it has big implications for the work we do with students. When we don't have diverse voices in the room, we tend to miss obvious blind spots.

Life, Literacy, and the Pursuit of Happiness

This is why it is so important to have as many voices as possible represented when making decisions. For those who are in charge of personnel decisions, one simple solution is to hire more people of color. On a national level, President Joe Biden took this advice when he made his Cabinet the most diverse in the history of the United States. Representation matters!

If your district is made up mainly of white educators, it is imperative to search for educators from different experiences and backgrounds. Your schools and community will benefit on many levels, including getting a variety of perspectives on programs and policies. Your students, whatever their race or ethnicity, will benefit from seeing a person of color as their teacher or principal. It will not only prepare them for the real world but also ensure positive experiences with people outside their culture. It will help them expand their bubbles.

My schools always had diverse teaching staffs. When hiring, I always look for highly qualified people of color, knowing that my students and faculty would be better for having learned from a teacher and colleague who represented the world outside of our school walls. That's not to say I didn't hire promising white women—I've hired plenty of them who have turned out to be some of our best teachers. But if you are truly committed to reimagining your schools for all children, diversity among the adults needs to be viewed as an asset and a non-negotiable.

If you are truly committed to reimagining your schools for all children, diversity among the adults needs to be viewed as an asset and a non-negotiable.

Commitment to Supporting Newcomers

Up to now, my discussion of commitment has mainly focused on improving our individual and collective selves as educators of all students. I'd like to shift that focus and reflect on how to support our immigrant and refugee students, keeping in mind the specific academic, social, and cultural needs that they possess, which must be addressed.

Whether you have one new immigrant or refugee student, or a large number of them, it's important to find ways to support them. One way to do that is with a newcomer program, which provides a critical bridge for your students and their families toward realizing the American Dream. According to Breiseth, Robertson, and Lafond (2011) and Castellón and her colleagues (2015), effective newcomer programs should have six areas of support for immigrant and refugee students and their families:

- A system to gather knowledge about the individual students and their needs;

- Structures to support their learning needs;

- Ways for effective communication between home and school (including language support);

- Opportunities for family engagement;

- Supports for cultural and language integration; and

- Opportunities for family and community partnerships.

Teachers in newcomer programs use literacy as a natural way to provide support to immigrant and refugee children. Picture books are an essential part of supporting emergent bilinguals in their target language development (more on that later), but they can be equally helpful in supporting newcomers' cultural integration.

One picture book you might consider using is Sarvinder Naberhaus's *Blue Sky White Stars* (illustrated by Caldecott winner Kadir Nelson). This book captures the richness of America from the perspective of our flag. With beautiful illustrations and few words, it provides a wonderful springboard for conversations about and lessons on American culture, history, and current events.

Picture books can also be used to address social and emotional needs, as newcomers find comfort in stories of other young immigrants and refugees who are in the same shoes they are in. *The Name Jar* by Yangsook Choi, for example, may be just right for a newcomer who is anxious about her American classmates being unable to pronounce her name. Stories can help heal (or at least start the process of healing) some of the trauma—big or small—that newcomers experience while transitioning to a new life.

Through literacy, you can also engage families, support them, and connect them to community resources. In our Parent Resource Center, for example, we provided multilingual children's books for parents to read with their children at home and information on the importance of reading at home with children. Think about making space (preferably near the front office) for parents to access information (properly translated into home languages) about the support that is available to them through your school or community organizations. You might include information on local libraries, social and health services, refugee resettlement programs, and religious and cultural organizations. Of course, it is important to make families aware of this information by holding newcomer parent meetings or initiating some kind of PTA outreach.

PURSUIT OF COMMITMENT

Get to Know Your Students

In *Being the Change: Lessons and Strategies to Teach Social Comprehension* (2018), Sara K. Ahmed introduces the idea of Identity Webs, graphic tools for students and teachers to explore their identities and connect with others' identities. She dedicates the first chapter of the book to ideas for students to explore and affirm their own identities, providing lessons that guide teachers in this work.

In one lesson, she explains how to use mentor texts to help students write stories of how they got their names and how their names are an important part of their identity. This strategy is especially helpful to newcomers who may feel uneasy about their non-English names and need to be reassured that everyone's name should be honored and respected, regardless of how uncommon it is.

Many immigrant and refugee students have poignant family stories to tell that are testaments of courage, resilience, and faith. In another lesson, Ahmed has students explore their identities by sharing their family histories, artifacts, and heirlooms, as well as stories passed from generation to generation. Using the structure of George Ella Lyon's poem, "Where I'm From," students write their own poems about their family's history.

Finally, throughout *Being the Change*, Ahmed provides great recommendations of children's books, poems, essays, and anthologies for you to use to enrich learning and discovery.

Getting parents to attend meetings can be a challenge. And it can be especially hard getting immigrant and refugee parents to attend because of the cultural and language barriers. It's not impossible, though. A few years ago, my colleagues and I were struggling to get parents to attend our ELAC (English Language Acquisition Committee) meetings. And it was no wonder, because those meetings were not much more than boring rundowns of parent notifications and presentations on school and government mandates. I didn't even want to attend! Most of the time, only two parents showed up—the same two.

So Mary Vanderleun, one of our ELAC coordinators, and I decided to stop wasting time and make the meeting more meaningful for parents—and it worked! By the end of the school year, we had hosted several ELAC meetings, with over 30 parent attendees at each one, which changed the way we planned future meetings. Here are some recommended actions for involving families in school meetings based on what worked at our school:

Schools need to commit fully to supporting newcomers and their families in navigating the academic, social, and cultural challenges they face. Literacy can play a huge role in that effort.

Invite parents. Call them on the phone or tell them when you see them on campus. This personal touch makes a difference. If there's a language barrier, have a translator available.

Have food. Food is always important for any parent meeting!

Read aloud a children's book. It's a great way to start a meeting and it gives you an opportunity to model and discuss the importance of reading aloud books at home.

Ask attendees what they want for their kids and what they need from you. Encourage honest feedback and allow them to voice their hopes and dreams for their children's future. Take good notes and be sure to follow up on any questions or concerns that you couldn't address in the meeting. Make sure you allocate money for immigrant and refugee programs and activities and prioritize their needs. (You may have funding available that is specifically reserved for those families.)

Share resources. Seize this opportunity to share with the parents information about community organizations, school materials (multilingual books, computers, videos), and other resources that can help them and their children. And make sure you explain how to access and use those resources!

If parents feel they and their families are respected and valued, then they will drop everything to be on campus to meet with you. Of course, the opposite is also true, especially with families of newcomers where social and cultural barriers can discourage them from visiting the campus. Schools need to commit fully to supporting newcomers and their families in navigating the academic, social, and cultural challenges they face. Literacy can play a huge role in that effort. The American Dream—no matter the interpretation of it—can be realized by all newcomers if we commit to lifting them up in our schools as they begin their journey in America.

PURSUIT OF COMMITMENT

Rethink Professional Development

Oakland International High School (OIHS) in Oakland, California, has been serving immigrant and refugee students and families for more than a decade and a half. A few years ago, administrators there decided to focus teacher in-service days on developing a better understanding of its students and their families and building stronger relationships with them. Every year, teachers and staff go on a "Community Walk" to get a better sense of where and how students live. On the walk, designed by parents, students, and community leaders, OIHS teachers and staff spend the day touring the neighborhood and talking to all stakeholders in the community. They are shown important landmarks and cultural centers, meet with community leaders and advocates, and listen to student presentations. From visiting a mosque to having a family lunch to touring a local youth and family shelter, the teachers and staff truly learn about the kids and families they serve. Discussion topics include students' backgrounds, families' hopes, and challenges newcomers are facing in the community. Lauren Markham, one of the coordinators of the event, says, "The Community Walks are a beloved tradition at OIHS. It's powerful to give students and families the mic to teach their teachers what it is that they wish the staff better understood about their communities, homes, identities, lived experiences, and personal and collective histories."

Commitment to Changing

It's time to move our schools from being compliant to being committed. The movement starts with us looking within ourselves to be the change makers in our schools. The opportunities for change are right before us, right now. Let's commit to change. Let's build a new era in schools where the pursuit of happiness and the American Dream is within the grasp of all kids.

PURSUIT OF COMMITMENT

Check Out These Newcomer Resources for Educators

The Newcomer Toolkit (U.S. Department of Education) provides educators with comprehensive school and classroom resources to help immigrants and refugees with their educational, legal, and social-emotional needs. It includes information on partnerships with families and showcases newcomer programs throughout the country that have been successful in helping new students and families thrive.

The National Child Traumatic Stress Network (NCTSN) provides information on many resources for refugee children and the impact of trauma. On this website, you can find basic definitions of refugee trauma, screening and assessment resources, interventions, and links to external partners and organizations that may provide support and care for refugee and immigrant children.

The U.S. Committee for Refugees and Immigrants provides a list with links to 100 agencies that operate in service of immigrants and refugees for various needs. From surviving human trafficking to assisting unaccompanied minors, an interactive map will help you or families you serve find assistance. Their website also is translated into several languages, including Spanish, Arabic, and Ukrainian.

For free access and links to these websites and resources, go to scholastic.com/LifeLiteracyResources.

This photo was taken a few months after we arrived in America in 1975. (I'm the unhappy one in the red hoodie.)

NEW HORIZONS

THE REFUGEE EXPERIENCE IS A GREAT EQUALIZER for many. No matter who you were in your previous life, no matter how connected or how wealthy you were, leaving your homeland for a new country means starting over. For some, that means a second chance to make a better life. For others, that means losing everything. My wife's father, a high-ranking police officer while living in Vietnam, wound up working in an American factory before a debilitating stroke forced him to stay home for his remaining years of life. His wife, on the other hand, was orphaned as a young child, left Vietnam with no money and family, and took full advantage of opportunities offered to her in the United States. Regardless of one's past, everyone is in the same boat, figuratively and literally (or the same airplane, in my family's case).

At the end of the Vietnam War in 1975, Camp Pendleton, the Marine Corps base in southern California, was turned into a processing center for thousands of Southeast Asian refugees waiting to be sponsored by families or charitable organizations for resettlement into communities throughout the country. So it was fitting that the officials there gave this resettlement operation the code name "New Horizons." Over only a couple of days, the Marines created a tent city, laying down plywood floors, putting up sleeping cots, and building restrooms and other basic infrastructure essentials for the initial wave of over a thousand refugees. This number swelled to over 5,000 by the week's end. By November of that year, more than 50,000 refugees had passed through Camp Pendleton. My family was included in the first group of shell-shocked and bewildered Vietnamese who had not only just lost a war, but also lost a country.

Life in Camp Pendleton was surprisingly pleasant. The seven of us— myself, my parents, brother, cousin, and two grandmothers—were assigned to a corner of a Quonset hut, a steel structure shaped like a half cylinder laid on its diameter, along with about 30 other refugees. We considered ourselves lucky because these huts quickly filled up and, once they did, people were sent to live in the less comfortable tents down the road. There were several families in our hut—people of all ages and from all walks of life.

One particular family would take turns bringing the patriarch food throughout the day. The man, who was probably in his fifties and not ill or frail, kept to himself and refused to leave the hut except to use the restroom. It was only after he and his family had left the camp that my parents discovered he had served as a general in the South Vietnamese Army. My parents suspected he felt ashamed of leading in a war, losing ground, and ultimately fleeing the country that he was protecting.

Life, Literacy, and the Pursuit of Happiness

Or maybe his despair stemmed from going from a powerful position to a powerless one.

The Marines made every effort to make life comfortable for us new Americans. We were given three meals a day, American movies in the evening, and lectures and classes intended to help us assimilate into American culture as quickly as possible. Military-issued cots, blankets, and even clothes were provided. Parents of infants were given disposable diapers—a luxury that was unheard of in Vietnam. The clothes issued were too big for most of the smaller-framed Vietnamese, so the women started using the bedsheets as fabric to make their own shirts and pants. The Marines didn't mind the ingenuity and, in fact, found more sheets for them.

After a few weeks of eating flavorless foreign food in the mess hall, the refugees requested fish sauce. (In case you're not a foodie, fish sauce is an essential ingredient in Vietnamese cuisine.) Because there was nowhere to find fish sauce in America at that time, the Marines had bottles of it shipped from Thailand. By most accounts, the Marines at Camp Pendleton represented the goodness and promise of America. They saw their fellow humans in need and did what they could to help.

Every morning, my father would walk over to the central information office (which was located in another Quonset hut) to see if our family was on the list to be sponsored for resettlement. He knew it was going to be difficult because of our family's size. Many sponsors—whether charitable organizations or individual families—did not have the resources to provide for a family as large as ours, so they chose ones with fewer members.

As he took his walk every morning, my father would dream about the future in America. With my mother, he had just purchased a house in Saigon the week before leaving. He had a good job at the U.S. Embassy that he knew disappeared the instant the American flag was lowered there. It was in Camp Pendleton that his hope for a better future began to overshadow the loss of the past. He didn't know much about America except that he heard it was one of the greatest countries in the world. What he knew he learned from the Friday night movies that played at the local community center near the U.S. Embassy. He watched them all. He remembered scenes from New York City. What country could build so many skyscrapers that touched the clouds? Only America. How magnificent was the Statue of Liberty? Very magnificent, but not as magnificent as the words at her feet. He thought, "Here we are. The tired. The poor. The homeless." He remembered movies featuring American citizens in their beautiful homes, driving their beautiful cars down their beautiful highways. Just like in the movies, he imagined driving his own fancy car someday, the windows rolled down, the cool breeze blowing his hair, as he sped down the highway. The promise of America meant that his family would live a better life than the one he had left behind in Vietnam, especially now that the communists had taken over. My parents, with my grandmothers, prayed the rosary every night in that Quonset hut for a sponsor to find us our new home. But as time passed, and other families left and new ones arrived, my parents wondered if their turn would ever come.

Their prayers were finally answered after three months, when the United States Catholic Conference (USCC) sponsored my family, along with several other families, to resettle in the Central Valley of California. We were all placed in a temporary multifamily home called Samaritan House, a former nursing home. Community volunteers helped us settle into our new lives by finding us permanent homes, finding us jobs, enrolling us in English as a Second Language (ESL) classes, and getting the kids into schools.

For the first three months at Samaritan House, my parents worked odd jobs and saved enough money to buy a beat-up light-green Cadillac from one of the community volunteers for $500. My dad finally got his fancy American car—his friends in Vietnam would be so amused that a refugee was driving a Cadillac! A few weeks after that, my parents found an apartment and we moved out of Samaritan House. On November 11, 1975, my father found a job as an electrician across town and, with that, we were on our own to pursue the American Dream.

The typical refugee success story is a myth. The idea that one man or woman, through hustle, hard work, and courage can overcome odds to create a better life for him- or herself in a new country can lead us all to believe that refugees are the only ones responsible for whether they succeed or not. Yes, it's true that it takes an extraordinary amount of hustle, hard work, and courage to thrive in a new country. But many refugees have pursued success and failed.

The success of refugees, immigrants, and anyone less fortunate in society depends upon the support and care of others. My parents were twentysomething newlyweds who were just starting their lives together. Like many of the Vietnamese refugees at the time, they were ordinary people who found themselves in an extraordinary situation. It took courage for them to leave and to start again. It took ingenuity and resilience to find a new way to survive and live. And it took hope and faith to dream a better life for themselves and their children. But they couldn't have done it alone.

I wouldn't be telling this story if it weren't for the Marines at Camp Pendleton who had taken such good care of my family and others. The men and women who trained to fight the war became our caretakers after the war. I wouldn't be telling this story if it weren't for the many charitable organizations and individual citizens who sponsored the hundreds of thousands of new refugees, strangers from a different shore, and opened their homes and communities to them. I wouldn't be telling this story if it weren't for the people who saw a need—from taking a chance on a refugee and giving him a job or helping to enroll her children in school—and offered a helping hand.

I feel especially fortunate because helping Vietnamese resettle wasn't the popular thing to do at that time in America. According to a Gallup poll in May 1975, only 36 percent of Americans approved of allowing Vietnamese refugees to resettle here (Stern, 1981). Even Cesar Chavez and the United Farm Workers opposed mass immigration from Vietnam, fearing the influx of refugees would impact the jobs and wages of California farm workers. Those who opposed the majority opinion, and acted on their convictions to help the refugees, changed the trajectory of many lives, including mine.

In our communities and schools today, we can see the same story unfolding. There is still a debate—from the family dinner table to the highest offices in government—on whether refugees and immigrants deserve a place in America. Yet, migration continues. U.S. Census data show that over 20 percent of all students in America are foreign born or have at least one foreign-born parent. By 2030, approximately 40 percent of all children in American schools, many of whom will be born outside the country, will learn English as a new language (Shah, 2012).

In addition to immigrants and refugees, we have an unprecedented number of students who suffer from poverty. A UNICEF (2017) report found one in five American children live in conditions that fall below the poverty line and are unsure where they will get their next meal. According to the USDA (2017), over 30 million students in America receive free and reduced-price lunches because they cannot afford to feed themselves.

We are all called to our profession because we know how much of an impact educators can have on the lives of children and their families. We teach, we support, and we do everything we can to help those in our care. Providing our new, striving, and disenfranchised students with a lifelong love of literacy is one way we can make a difference in their lives. Literacy offers our students and their families greater access and the ability to achieve in all areas of life—it is a key to freedom and one way we can help them succeed in their pursuit of the American Dream.

CLOCK

"Books are the plane, and the train, and the road. They are the destination, and the journey. They are home."

—ANNA QUINDLEN

For many refugees and immigrants, the importance of learning and using English in America can vary, depending on their generation. My grandparents, for example, never learned to speak English, and they lived fairly comfortable lives here. They were much older than the rest of us and spent their days taking care of their grandchildren, cooking and cleaning at home, and going to church on Sundays. None of those activities required English. (At church, they would recite to themselves the traditional prayers in Vietnamese.)

On the other hand, my parents, like many refugee and immigrant adults in their twenties, learned early on that literacy was key to their survival and success in America. They needed English to navigate their daily lives—going to the doctor, getting groceries, speaking with coworkers, and watching the news. They also knew that literacy was going to be just as important, if not more important, for the next generation of Americans in the family. The fact that their children were going to be able to start school and learn English from an early age meant they would not only survive, but also thrive in a way that my parents could never imagine. With hard work, perseverance, and determination, immigrant and refugee children can become anything in this country except for President of the United States. Everything else is possible.

For children to become fulfilled and productive citizens and assume their place in America, they must come out of school with the ability to read, write, and speak in English. Acquisition of English allows them to access academic subjects, it allows them to access the culture, and it gives them opportunities in life that non-English speakers in America will never have. Given that many refugee and immigrant children come from homes where English isn't spoken fluently, it is imperative for schools to provide an environment where they can not only learn and use English, but also develop a lifelong love of reading.

With that being said, let us also keep in mind that our immigrant and refugee students come to us with language skills and cultural capital from their prior homeland—assets we can use in our teaching. In *Rooted in Strength: Using Translanguaging to Grow Multilingual Readers and Writers*, Cecilia Espinosa and Laura Ascenzi-Moreno (2021) remind us:

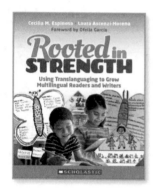

> Far too often, emergent bilinguals are asked to wait until their English is good enough to fully engage in the transformative vision for reading and writing that we aim to provide for all students. Or they are asked to leave key aspects of their language repertoire at the classroom door. Emergent bilinguals' language differences, cultural resources, and educational histories are often seen as challenges, rather than assets in their learning.

In other words, we can't wait until their English is "good enough." To best serve our emergent bilinguals, we must continually create opportunities for all of our students to engage in deep thinking so that they can be fully present in our classrooms. We must meet them where they are, in any language, and use their unique assets of culture and language to enrich our teaching and learning.

The condition of "Clock" is a reference to the idea that this effort requires time—including the time to read together and independently. If schools can create an environment that prioritizes providing students time to read on campus and at home, our immigrant and refugee students have better opportunities to thrive and succeed.

Life, Literacy, and the Pursuit of Happiness

The Importance of Independent Reading

Where do we start in creating that environment? Many schools use core reading programs and interventions to develop students' fundamental language skills. Those programs and interventions are important because they provide a systematic approach to addressing the needs of students. However, that is only half the work. What good is it to teach kids how to read if they don't like to read, and end up never choosing to read? Encouraging independent reading, and developing a love of it, is an essential part of any literacy program. After all, how are students ever going to get better at reading if they don't practice it at school and home?

Paul Bambrick-Santoyo of Uncommon Schools, among many other prominent educators, suggests that we shouldn't expect kids to become independent adult readers if they haven't read independently in school, arguing:

> If guided reading is about coaching and practicing with young readers, then independent reading is about sending them into a crucial scrimmage. So, what's the 'big game' they're preparing for? A lifetime of both academic and extracurricular reading adventures: analyzing primary history sources, reviewing the findings of laboratory reports, or just picking up novels for pleasure. Students aren't ready for that unless they can engage in independent reading in the classroom—that is, unless they are able to read successfully when the teacher steps back to the sidelines, when they must use their whole inventory of essential reading skills at once (Bambrick-Santoyo, Settles, & Worrell, 2013).

Independent reading is invaluable to all students, particularly our refugee and immigrant students, who may not have English support at home.

Independent reading is invaluable to all students, particularly our refugee and immigrant students, who may not have English support at home, nor the resources to make books available at home. They also may not have the time and space at home to read.

How important is independent reading to the growth and success of students? The quick answer is, of course, a lot. The more you practice something, the better you get at it, right? We don't need Malcolm Gladwell to tell us that it takes 10,000 hours of deliberate practice to get really good at something.

However, when we study the educational research on the volume of independent reading and the impact it has on student reading achievement, it is crystal clear that the more students read, the more proficient they become.

- According to John Guthrie and his colleagues (2012), students who read widely and frequently are more proficient readers than students who rarely read. This is evident regardless of socioeconomic background.

- Lucy Calkins and her colleagues (2012) state, "Students who read a lot score a lot better on every imaginable test—the NAEP, the SAT, and the ACT. One of the best ways of doing this is to allow students to read habitually, and in ways that literate people the world over read."

- Anderson, Wilson, and Fielding (1988) concluded, "For virtually all children, the amount of time spent reading in classrooms consistently accelerates their growth in reading skills."

- The volume of independent reading students do in school is significantly related to their gains in reading achievement (Allington, 2012; Cunningham & Stanovich, 2003; Guthrie, 2004; Hiebert & Reutzel, 2010; Swan et al., 2010).

Students who clock nine minutes of independent reading each school day will read about 601,000 words in a typical school year. Those students usually score in the 50th percentile on standardized reading tests. In other words, just a slight increase in time spent reading can produce substantial results. In fact, students who clock about 25 minutes more a day read about 2.4 million words a year and score in the 90th percentile on the same standardized tests (Anderson, Wilson, & Fielding, 1988).

When it comes to socioeconomics, independent reading in school plays an even more critical role. Children from lower-income homes often

Minutes matter when it comes to independent reading.

do most of their independent reading at school because they either don't have the books or don't have adults around who can read to them. Allocating time for independent reading in school helps all students—but it is imperative for students who come to us from lower-income homes. And, usually, our immigrant and refugee students fall into that category.

Even though the research on the importance of independent reading in schools is robust, only 36 percent of classroom teachers report that they allocate time for students to read independently every day and 23 percent don't allocate any time at all (Scholastic Teacher & Principal School Report, 2017). We can't blame teachers for those percentages, though, given the demands they're under. Teachers are overwhelmed trying to keep up with the pacing guides, required curriculum, standardized testing, and so forth, so that finding time to have kids read independently is a major challenge. If schools and districts are committed to building a culture of literacy for all, then putting structures in place to give time for students to read must be part of that commitment.

If schools and districts are committed to building a culture of literacy for all, then putting structures in place to give time for students to read must be part of that commitment.

Finding Time for Reading in School

Imagine this scenario. You're a teacher, and you decide to provide time for your students to read independently after recess. In the middle of independent reading time, your principal unexpectedly walks into your classroom for an informal observation. What's the first thing that goes through your mind? You know independent reading is important, but a side of you feels guilty that your students are "just reading." Are you fearful your principal feels the instructional time is being wasted? Now imagine that you are that principal. How do you feel? Is there a side of you that wishes the students were engaged in something else? Are you thinking the time would be better spent covering standards before the annual state tests? Whether you're the teacher or the principal, it's understandable to feel anxiety. Nevertheless, I propose that we shift our priorities and commit to the idea that independent reading time is not only an acceptable practice in schools, but also an essential practice.

What Independent Reading Is—and Isn't

First, let's be clear on what independent reading isn't: It's not D.E.A.R. (Drop Everything And Read) time. Some people have the wrong idea that independent reading time is free reading time that is not guided by the teacher. Yes, students should have control over and choice in what they read, but you should have a clear idea of what each student is reading and how to support him or her.

Now, let's talk about what independent reading is: It should be an integral part of any school's reading program. Independent reading should be a joyous time for students to explore their interests by reading books, magazines, or online material on their own. It provides students with much needed reading practice. It also helps them develop a positive relationship with reading—a relationship that, I hope, will last a lifetime.

Despite its name, independent reading should not be done independently from the teacher. You are critical in planning and directing independent reading time so that all students benefit from it. Some students may need your assistance to find the right book at an appropriate level. Use independent reading time to conference with individual students about what they are reading and how to plan their reading time.

At Barrett Ranch, our teacher teams used independent reading time as an opportunity for students to rotate through a variety of literacy-related experiences. Following the Daily 5/CAFE literacy framework of the "sisters" Gail Boushey and Joan Moser (2014), students read to classmates, engaged in word work, wrote, and listened to reading. The teacher would situate herself at one of the centers, teaching a specific reading skill or doing guided reading with a group of students. This small-group instruction time was especially beneficial to our large number of emergent bilinguals. Of course, one of the centers was "reading to self," where students would engage in silent, self-selected reading. In the past few years, inspired by the work coming out of the Teachers College Reading and Writing Project, we've moved toward integrating parts of Reading Workshop into our instruction. This model also places great emphasis on the role of independent reading that is guided by the teacher through individual and small-group discussions to meet the students where they are, develop their reading skills, and cultivate their passion for reading (Calkins, 2015).

Decide What Independent Reading Looks Like in Your School

Knowledge workers are defined as people who work in fields requiring the exchange and use of knowledge. Educators fall into this category. Peter Drucker, Simon Sinek, Daniel Pink, and other thought leaders in the field of leadership and management have explored the unique aspects of working with knowledge workers. To make meaningful change, knowledge workers need to know and understand the "why" of the work—its purpose. And it's equally important to remember to revisit regularly the "why" of your own work (Pink, 2011; Sinek, Mead, & Docker, 2017). Why do you want students to read independently at school? Here's what I suggest.

1. Meet as a leadership team and discuss the benefits of independent reading. What does the research say about it? How does it help students to be successful in school and after they move on? Why is it especially important to students who may not have opportunities to read independently at home?

2. Determine what is already happening on campus to support independent reading time. Are there practices to expand or eliminate? What are the best strategies being implemented and how can the staff learn from them and grow together?

3. If independent reading is not happening, figure out how to carve out 30 minutes for it during the school day. Remember, it is not an add-on, but rather an integral part of a robust ELA curriculum. It must become a priority in your school. Allocating time to it will be evidence of your commitment.

4. Discuss how you will support emergent bilingual, immigrant, and refugee students during independent reading time. What resources are needed to support those students?

5. Develop an implementation plan for schoolwide independent reading. You may roll it out one grade level at a time, but be sure, within a reasonable amount of time, students in all grades, from all language backgrounds, are spending time in their day reading on their own.

Finding Time for Reading After School

Many schools provide opportunities for students to extend learning beyond regular school hours, and provide much-needed childcare for families. Many programs are offered at no cost (supported through grants and government funds) and provide academic assistance to students who need to make up for lost time.

If you haven't done so already, why not add independent reading to your after-school program? It wouldn't cost anything and would give kids a joyful, peaceful time to decompress from the day.

You can run the after-school program the way you run independent reading time during school, with the teacher working with individual students or small groups of students while the rest of the class reads independently. You can also enlist the help of community volunteers who may be more available to help after school—parents, grandparents, and high school students looking for service hours. "You're at school picking up your brother? Why not stay an extra 30 minutes and help in our after-school reading program?" How great would it be for young students to have an older student read to them and discuss books with them after school? If you're looking to expand your circle of readers to include family and community members, after-school programs are a great way to do it.

Libraries

Is the room with the school's biggest collection of books being used in after-school programs? Many schools don't open the library after school because there's no funding available or no staff member willing to supervise. But imagine if the library was a part of an after-school program and kids were allowed to browse books and read independently there. They could check out books or not. What's important is that they spend some quiet time reading and enjoying books, rather than worrying about the next class or upcoming quiz. The joy of reading just may be ignited there.

You can also inquire about the after-school programs that are already in place at your local public library and find ways to collaborate with librarians there to tailor the program to meet your students' needs and desires. After all, public libraries want kids and families reading more. They serve the same population as you do, so it's a no-brainer to work together on that common goal. They have additional resources, such as funding (although not as much as they deserve), personnel, and, most likely, a larger collection of books.

Imagine if all school and community libraries were open to kids after hours.

Finding Time for Reading at Home

What can you do to encourage independent reading at home? First, make sure students have access to books because, obviously, if students are going to read independently at home, they must have books inside the home. So be sure that they are able to borrow books from your classroom and school libraries. Provide them with opportunities to purchase books through classroom book clubs and school book fairs. Organize used-book sales and exchanges throughout the year so kids can find books to read and keep at little or no cost. Be sure they have access to the local public library and, if they don't, facilitate that connection.

Once you know that students have something to read at home, how do you get them and their families to set aside time to read? Start by providing parents with the information about the importance of reading independently, as well as together as a family. In a meeting or communication (preferably both), present to parents the research described in this chapter about the benefits of independent reading and reading aloud with kids. The more parents know about how children become better readers and the more they see their own children experiencing reading success in school, the more likely they will be to set aside reading time at home.

Meet the Needs of New Waves of Refugees

Almost five million refugees have fled Syria since the beginning of a brutal civil war in 2011 that has left hundreds of thousands of people dead. According to the State Department's Refugee Processing Center, the United States resettled approximately 18,000 Syrian refugees from 2011 to the beginning of 2017 (U.S. Department of State, 2020).

While the Syrian diaspora spreads across many states, a large percentage of refugees settled in California after the war. In 2016, the Cajon Valley Union School District, located near San Diego, admitted 76 new Syrian refugee students into their schools, and that number has increased every year since. Today, the district serves almost 6,000 emergent bilinguals, and half of them speak Arabic.

District leaders and staff members at Cajon Valley formed the Family and Community Engagement (FACE) office to support school communities in their efforts to connect with refugee families. They created a "parent university" at each Title I school to address the needs of parents, with a focus on literacy at home. Teachers and community liaisons give parent presentations on how to read with children at home—modeling what it looks like and suggesting questions to ask. They also send home children's books in English and Arabic that they purchased with grant money. The director of the district's FACE office, Michael Serban, says, "The key is to educate parents so they become a voice for their child at home. But they're not going to read at home just because we say they should. How many times have you done something that someone you don't completely trust told you to do? Probably not too many! A parent will only do it if we build a relationship and trust. We took several weeks to reach out, build connections, and get to know the families." Considering that many of those families left their homeland with little trust in their government, building trust was critical to the success of Cajon Valley's initiative.

If the parents of your refugee and immigrant students don't speak or read English, encourage them to choose books or material online in their primary language and read them with their kids. This not only ensures that kids have quality time with their parents, it also gives them a reading role model and celebrates their primary language and culture.

Don't forget to take inventory of the bilingual books in your school and make them available to families. You can also guide families to bilingual collections at the public library. Making available multilingual and multicultural titles that reflect the diversity of your families will build a bridge from school to home.

Finding Time for Reading During Summer

I remember going to the Manteca Public Library a lot as a kid during the summer, and it was cool. And I don't mean figuratively cool. It was literally cool. The central valley of California can get hot during the summer, and air conditioning in our home was a luxury for my Vietnamese refugee family. So I spent much of my summer reading in the library and exploring the world of books. In the process, I learned a lot about the world itself and built critical background knowledge.

Today, families with resources often send their kids to summer camps—science camp, art camp, etc. There's even a Harry Potter camp—how cool would going there be?! Kids from those families typically have access to books at home and in the community. They can spend summers continuing to learn, developing skills, and building background knowledge that is critical to their academic and social development.

Teachers Mary and Jamie getting ready for a read-aloud.

Unfortunately, many students who come from less privileged backgrounds don't have the same opportunities. Their families may not have the resources to send them to summer camps. According to research, students from low-income communities have access to far fewer books than students from high-income communities (Neuman & Celano, 2001; 2012). As a result, our socioeconomically disadvantaged students (including our immigrant and refugee students) show little to no growth during the summer. And some of them lose one to three months of learning (Cooper et al., 2000; Kim, 2009). That is known as the "summer slide," and every summer, our most needy students slide further and further behind.

The good news is that we can help our students avoid the summer slide and continue their learning over the summer. When I was a principal, I made it a priority to get books into kids' hands over the summer months. Research tells us that sending books home during the summer boosts achievement and is less expensive than traditional summer school programs (Allington & McGill-Franzen, 2013; McGill-Franzen et al., 2016).

My colleagues and I created a summer reading program called "Summer on the Ranch," which opened up the school library to students for the entire summer. Why not? We had the books, after all. Why leave them sitting in the library collecting dust all summer? We also tied the library program to our free summer lunch program (funded through a federal grant). Families dropped off kids at the library in the morning for a couple of hours to read or be read to. After that, they picked up a free lunch in the cafeteria and went home. It was pretty simple. We used Title I money to pay a few staff members and for some books to give away. We didn't let the kids check out books because we didn't have the personnel to manage circulation, but that was okay because it encouraged students to come back the next day to continue their reading. In addition to

An advertisement for our summer reading program that we sent out to all families. It was also translated into major languages.

Life, Literacy, and the Pursuit of Happiness

Provide Books to Kids During the Summer

Bellevue Elementary School is located in a semirural area of Santa Rosa, California. It serves a low socioeconomic community made up of over 80 percent Hispanic families, many of whom are immigrants. Most parents work in the farming or service industry and almost all of their children participate in the free and reduced-price school lunch program. Retired teacher and principal Nancy Rogers-Zegarra and the Gateway Reading Council received a grant to provide every K–3 student in the school with a summer reading package that included several books of his or her choice. The package also included information for parents on reading together over the summer, accessing ebooks, and preventing the summer slide. Dr. Rogers-Zegarra says, "Since the community doesn't have a library nearby, it was important for us to give children access to books over the summer. We worked with the city library to provide them with ebooks, but many of the families didn't have the technology necessary to use them. So we worked as a community to find them Chromebooks and Internet hotspots. It's still a struggle, but we are working hard to ensure that the kids don't fall further behind."

reading to kids in person, we read to them online, and we made sure they knew the hours of our local public libraries.

Letting kids read and borrow books is helpful, but research shows that giving books to kids for their personal libraries significantly improves their reading achievement. In fact, students who receive and read books over the summer experience the equivalent of attending three years of summer school (Allington & McGill-Franzen, 2013). The impact of owning books is real for our students.

While providing access to books during the summer is critical in preventing the summer slide, it's not good enough. After all, just because you put a book in a student's hands doesn't mean he or she will read it. That's why, when planning summer reading, make sure it's an extension of reading that happens—and students enjoy—during the school year. In other words, your summer reading program should be a continuation of your reading program.

Here are some questions you may want to discuss as a team to ensure that kids read the books you provide them over the summer.

- Are we creating conditions that foster a love of reading in our students?
- Do we have books available in our school that our students are interested in reading?
- Are our students reading for pleasure?
- Are they given the chance to read independently at school? How are we supporting independent reading at home?
- How are we engaging our socioeconomically disadvantaged students?
- How are we engaging our emergent bilingual students?
- What about our refugee and immigrant families who may have cultural and language issues that need to be addressed?

Getting kids to read more and more deeply during the summer can't start at the beginning of summer vacation. It's a gradual and continuous process that starts when the school year starts. If students are reading for fun in their classrooms and at home, and are engaged in stories and other genres throughout the year, it shouldn't stop at the end of the school year. Summer can be an exciting time to explore, learn, and grow. Planning for the summer starts now.

The Clock Starts Now

According to the National Council of Teachers of English (NCTE) (2019), "Independent reading leads to an increased volume of reading. The more one reads, the better one reads." As research states, it is imperative that we find time for students to read. They need to read in school. They need to read after school. They need to read at home. And they need to read during the summer when they're away from us for weeks at a time. Time spent reading benefits all students. For immigrant and refugee students especially, that time is critical to their success in school and life. Many of those students have already lost valuable independent reading time because of life circumstances. Creating a culture of literacy in schools requires us to find the time to allow all students to read independently and with one another.

My mom at her first and only job in America.

AN ODE TO THE SUPERMARKET

TWO THINGS WERE EARTH-SHATTERING AND perspective-breaking to my parents as new refugees in America. First, they were shocked to see white people working in blue-collar jobs. They couldn't believe their eyes when they first spotted one working at a fast-food restaurant chain or sweeping floors at a local store. They would look at each other and giggle because it was such a ludicrous sight. Back in Vietnam, the few white people that they saw on a daily basis were either soldiers in the war or supervisors at companies. They never worked in retail. They were never seen doing manual labor. But they were in America.

The second thing that jarred them was supermarkets. They were in awe of the fact that American markets were so big and clean—that they had everything one ever needed or wanted under one roof. You want tomatoes in a can? Yes. How do you want them? Crushed, diced, whole, halved, or sauced? Which of the 10 available brands on the shelves are the best? In Vietnam, most people still shop at busy outdoor food stands. Picture a farmer's market on steroids with chaotic scenes of shoppers and vendors haggling over prices while scooters and cars zip by on the road. You want tomatoes? You'll get them just one way. Every vendor has a specialty, and you can spend most of the morning buying food for the day by visiting a variety of different stands.

It was different in America. Everything was under one roof. Shoppers used carts that glided on polished floors, browsed aisles and aisles of every food you could imagine, and even had the luxury of listening to soft music playing in the background. In a strange way, the supermarket became a symbol of American prosperity for my parents.

It's nothing short of poetic (or ironic) that my mom's first and only job in America was at a supermarket. After about a year in America, she had taken some ESL classes offered at the local resettlement organization and was able to speak some basic English—enough to finally get a job. The same resettlement organization notified her that a local supermarket, Safeway, was looking for people to bag groceries and collect the grocery carts left in the parking lot. She needed the work. My father had been working as an electrician for a local company, but they were still trying to make ends meet, and another income would help them do that.

On the day of her interview, my mother stood in the parking lot of Safeway for quite some time, watching the shoppers go in and out. All white. She assumed all fluent in English. All of them belonged there—this was their country, not hers. She was clearly different and could barely speak the language. She felt more alien than ever before. The feeling that she really didn't belong there, or have a place in this country, resonated so deeply that day. This was not the way the

Vietnamese shopped, and she feared the manager would never hire a refugee who could barely speak English.

My mother skipped the interview and walked home with tears streaming down her face. When she got home, she went straight into her room, laid down on the bed, and began to think. She thought about her family. Her present. Her future. She thought about our journey across the sea and questioned where we truly belonged. We could not go back to Vietnam. This was our home now and, as she watched her two young boys playing in the yard, she decided that she would do whatever was necessary to make a life for her family in America. She went back to the supermarket for the interview and got the job.

Her first week of work was going well until a manager asked to see her after her shift. He quietly said to her, "Nguyet, you're doing a good job but you can't wear flip-flops to work when you're out pushing grocery carts. It's a safety issue." My mom remembers that conversation and thinking that the only shoes she owned were flip-flops. Yet another break in perspective. Everyone in Vietnam wore flip-flops. She went to the flea market the next day and bought some closed-toe shoes for work. All was good again.

About a year later, my mother's manager offered her a promotion to clerk, and she was definitely interested. It would mean more money. But she was hesitant because of her language limitations. It was easy enough bagging groceries and collecting shopping carts in the parking lot, but clerks needed to talk to people. In English. Her manager encouraged her, though, and believed in her ability to pick up the job quickly. He said, "Nguyet, you're a smart woman, and you've learned so much. You don't need to read or say everything perfectly. The only thing you need to read perfectly are the numbers you put into the cash register." Again, this was in the 1970s, when there were no scanners and clerks needed to memorize and input the price of every item in the store manually. My mother hesitated but knew that this was a strength. She was good with numbers and had a great memory. Back in Vietnam, as a kid, she helped her family sell at the market at a chaotic food stand. If she could do that, this would be a piece of cake. She nodded. Her manager smiled and said, "I know you can do this job." And she did.

She worked at Safeway for the next 33 years and recently retired from her first and only job in America.

Reflecting upon her experience, my mom told me that working in a supermarket as a clerk opened up the English language to her, but also American culture. In her decades of conversations with shoppers, she would learn what Americans traditionally served on holidays (up to then, she had no idea what a Thanksgiving turkey tasted like), what they did on the weekends, and what their hopes and dreams were for their children. If shoppers were interested, my mom would share her story and her culture with them. In the process, she realized similarities outweighed differences, and that she had a place in America. She recalls, "I stopped taking the ESL classes soon after I started working but learned to speak more English at Safeway than ever before. Working there also helped me realize what it means to be an American and what the American Dream meant to me and my family. This is why I always take a few moments to reflect and be grateful whenever I'm shopping in a supermarket. The supermarket changed my life, our lives."

CONVERSATION

"Good conversation is as stimulating as black coffee, and just as hard to sleep after."

—ANNE MORROW LINDBERGH

Just as conversations with shoppers in a supermarket helped my mother learn English and understand American culture, conversations in schools can do the same. They can help shape not only the language development of immigrant and refugee students, but also their understanding of a new culture through books and stories. In addition, conversations create a culture of literacy in schools that can be beneficial to all students.

Literate Conversations at School

Let's revisit our imaginary school from Chapter 3 where a strong culture of literacy permeates the campus and every classroom. What kinds of conversations did you hear among the teachers and students? Of course, you heard formal conversations that help students develop their language skills and meet academic standards. However, a closer look in the classrooms and hallways reveals casual conversations that can be just as important. When it comes to building literacy, both types of conversations are critical.

When we're engaged in a "literate conversation," we simply talk informally, deeply, and honestly about the books and stories we are reading. Studies have found that adding 5 to 10 minutes of literate conversation at school improves students' comprehension more than any other strategy. In other words, when students talk about what they are reading with their teacher and classmates, they understand more of what they are reading (Applebee et al., 2003; Nystrand, 2006). For our immigrant and refugee students, literate conversations are sometimes more accessible and productive than more formal ones because they provide an opportunity to not only develop language skills for academic success, but also to make social and cultural connections with others. How do you make room for and support these kinds of conversations in schools?

> *When we're engaged in a "literate conversation," we simply talk informally, deeply, and honestly about the books and stories we are reading.*

Book Clubs

Although Oprah popularized them in the 1990s, book clubs have been around practically as long as books themselves. After all, isn't a book club just a group of people reading a book together and meeting to talk about it? If you're looking for ways to have more literate conversations in your school, start a book club. Fountas and Pinnell call them "Comprehension Clubs" and make a case that they offer the support that emergent bilinguals and emerging readers need: time for text, talk, and teaching (2012). Book clubs are a natural for kids because they invite kids to come together around a shared interest in a book, without any top-down teaching or testing. Barrett Ranch second-grade teachers, Kendra Barrett and Wendy Sievers, decided to start "Breakfast Clubs." They would gather a group of students before school once a week to talk about a book that they were reading together. They would sit down with some breakfast goodies and talk informally about the story and its characters. Kendra says, "The purpose of the Breakfast Club is to promote both reading success and good times with books, while building a reading community. As one of my favorite authors, Kate DiCamillo, says, 'Stories connect us.'" How did we pay for Breakfast Clubs? We used Title I funds to purchase the sets of books and pay our teachers for their time. After the books were taken out of the Breakfast Club rotation, they would go into classroom libraries and/or the school library. If you don't have Title I funds, consider Book Fair rewards, grants, or possibly money from a PTA fundraiser. Of course, you will want to compensate teachers for their time. If you can't pay for personnel costs, find out if it's possible to make it an adjunct duty or let teachers substitute their book club time for assigned yard duty/supervision time. If there's a will, there's a way.

Sometimes, kids won't wait for us adults to get it together so they can meet to talk about books. If you've created a strong enough culture of reading, your students may be creative and determined enough and get together on their own. I was a proud principal when several of my third and fourth graders asked if they could start a book club. I had a few questions for them.

"When will you meet?" I asked. They responded, "We can meet at lunch."

"What will you read?" I asked. They responded, "We will bring our own books. It will be like we're doing book talks. And we'll talk about books that we're reading together."

"Who's going to supervise you?" I asked. They responded, "You are!"

Was there any other way to respond to this request other than "Okay!"? I let the kids meet in my conference room once a week while they had lunch. It was fun popping in and listening to their book recommendations and seeing how passionate they were. How much did this cost? Nothing, except a little bit of elbow grease when I had to pick up the occasional chicken nugget that fell to the floor during one of their lively discussions.

One last note on book clubs—when building a culture of literacy, let's not forget adults in the building. Staff book clubs are a fun and engaging way to build an adult community of readers. I'm not talking about professional book studies, where we look at our practices and discuss pedagogy and policy. I'm talking about books that are not necessarily related to education and invite discussion of topics related to life outside of schools. Staff book clubs are beneficial in many ways. They remind us that reading transcends our classroom and school walls. They remind us that reading is important to the soul and can expose us to new places and different ideas. They remind us that literacy is a gift for all.

Launch a Principal's Book Club

Dr. Alice Lee, principal of Richmond Street School, asked teachers to nominate kids who would benefit from being a part of a book club. Dr. Lee was interested in kids who weren't necessarily bookworms but were in need of connecting with others. She remembers, "There was this kid, David, who had just come from Mexico the year before, and he was having a hard time adjusting socially and making friends. He came every week and didn't miss a meeting because I think it was the one place he knew he belonged."

Richmond Street School is located in El Segundo, California, near Los Angeles, an upper-middle-class community with few immigrant and refugee students. For Dr. Lee, David was a reminder that cultural differences can have a huge impact on some children's academic and social lives. A book club with her in her office opened the door to positive social interactions that he wouldn't have had otherwise. Dr. Lee says, "For David and the others, it gave them a safe space, a community, to engage in books with their peers. It also gave them another adult whom they connected with. The conversations were not only academic but social." She adds that the book club helped others realize that reading was an important part of the school's culture. "We were setting the example that reading was going to be a priority for everyone, even the principal. That was very powerful." It was powerful for not only the students, but also for the teachers who eventually started their own book clubs and special reading activities.

Student Book Talks

Have you ever watched a movie or eaten at a restaurant that you loved so much, you couldn't wait to tell somebody else about it? If so, you probably also know the feeling of finishing a book and immediately thinking of somebody you would recommend it to. That's the idea behind book talks.

What do book talks look like in school? It's simple, really. A student tells classmates a little bit about a book he or she has read and loved, and discusses why it may be interesting to others. Book talks are not book reports, so the student should only take a couple of minutes and be sure to leave out any spoilers! You can set aside a few minutes for one student to do a book talk every day. If you have 25 students, that's a month's worth of book talks. In my experience, many kids do end up reading the books that their classmates recommend. If your school has morning announcements, choose a couple of students to do a book talk for the entire school and, afterward, be sure to acknowledge them for their courage and passion. Then ask over the intercom if there's anyone who has read a good book that they would like to recommend. I guarantee you that you'll have a few takers!

Book Trailers

Book talks are best done in person, with a live audience, to allow for conversation. When that isn't possible, a videotaped book talk—or book trailer—is another tool to use to engage students in literate conversations and get them reading more books. A video book trailer is pretty much what it sounds like—a book promotion that's captured on video. Marketers have figured out that customers are 64 percent more likely to buy a book if they watch a trailer that effectively promotes it (ComScore Marketing, 2009). While we aren't interested in selling books to kids, we certainly are interested in seeing more kids read books.

When we started doing book trailers at Barrett Ranch, we wanted to address a need of many of our underserved students—including our immigrant and refugee students. Those students, we found, typically didn't have enough background knowledge to comprehend what they were reading and make connections across subject matters. As usual, it comes down to economics. Instead of attending enrichment camps during the summer, they spent their vacation at home babysitting their younger siblings. Instead of traveling and visiting museums, their families had to save money to make ends meet. These missed opportunities to build background knowledge had a significant impact on our students. According to researchers, background knowledge plays a critical role in reading. Providing students with relevant facts and details related to subjects you're teaching them improves their comprehension and learning (Routman, 2014; Shanahan, 2012). As such, in our book trailers, we include facts and details so that students are not only excited to read a particular book, but also have a chance to build their background knowledge.

You're probably asking, can you really build background knowledge through a video? According to Robert Marzano (2004), real-life experiences build background knowledge, but so do virtual experiences, such as video. So, for example, when we did a book trailer for *The Lorax* by Dr. Seuss, we included some information about conservationism, conservationist John Muir, and Yosemite National Park. When we did one on *Charlotte's Web*, we included

Make a Video Book Trailer

Follow these guidelines to create your own book trailer.

1. Find a book that you love. If you truly love it, it will show on the video!

2. Determine what you want to say. What themes can you pull from it? Is there anything unique about the book? What background knowledge would be helpful to comprehend and enjoy this book to its fullest? What makes it interesting for kids? Is there any vocabulary that you may need to preview?

3. Write a script. Offer a hook—and an enticing opening! Give facts and details to build background knowledge. State what you love about the book. Don't give away the ending. And keep it short!

4. Record yourself on video. Always use landscape mode so the video fills the entire television or computer screen. Clear sound is important, so use a microphone if you have one.

5. Include pictures and photos to add interest. When using a Google image search, look for copyright-free images.

6. Include background music. Use the YouTube Audio Library for copyright-free music.

7. Make simple edits using free editing software, such as iMovie or Powtoon.

8. Upload to your YouTube channel. (If you don't have one, you can create one for free.) You will need an online platform for storing and sharing videos.

9. Share your trailer with others: your students, their parents, students of a different grade level, or your entire school community. Tweet it out! Post it on Facebook and/or YouTube!

some information about farm animals and state fairs. Using video to promote a book allows you to not only give a book talk to a large audience, but also build students' background knowledge. We found it an excellent way to begin literate conversations with students.

Here's a still from a book trailer I did for Kwame Alexander's *Surf's Up*. In it, I share some background knowledge on Hawaii, the history of surfing, and explain idioms like, "Batten down the hatches!"

Adult Advice

As you begin your efforts to create a culture of literacy for all, students may initially be surprised to see that their teachers and principal read children's books for fun. But once the culture takes root, they will expect nothing less from you. Some of the most powerful literate conversations begin with an adult recommending a book to students. That adult can be any adult on campus— custodians, cafeteria helpers, teachers, counselors, the principal. When every adult is seen as a reader, every student is likely to become one, too.

Morning Announcements

So how can adults encourage literate conversations and foster a love of reading in kids? Remember when you gave that awesome book talk as part of morning announcements? Well, wouldn't it be cool to have Mr. Vasiliy, the lead custodian, recommend a book to kids during the next morning announcement? Kids would go crazy. Don't be surprised if that book disappears from the library shelf for the next month, with kids putting it on hold for checkout.

"Hot Reads" Bulletin Board

Another idea to consider is a bulletin board for staff book recommendations. This idea comes from Steven Layne (2012), author of *Igniting a Passion for Reading*, who calls these recommendations "Hot Reads." I asked each staff member to post a book recommendation for the "Hot Reads" bulletin board— just a one-pager containing a photo of the book and a short blurb on why kids should read it. We put the board in our multipurpose room so kids could read the latest recommendations as they lined up for lunch or gathered for an assembly. At the beginning of each new trimester, we refreshed the "Hot Reads" bulletin board with new recommendations.

A side note: A few years ago, Steven Layne came to Barrett Ranch for a professional development reading workshop, and I showed him our "Hot Reads" bulletin board. His jaw dropped and he beamed with pride as he took out his camera for a few selfies. It was one of my favorite memories as principal of Barrett Ranch.

Steven Layne, the inspiration for our "Hot Reads" bulletin board, checks it out himself!

Staff Recommendations

Finally, do you ever go to the "staff recommendations" section at the bookstore to see what the in-house experts have to say about books to read? Under each recommended book, there's usually a handwritten note about it by a staff member, explaining why he or she loves it so much. Well, why can't you do the same in your school library? Teachers and staff members can write up their recommendations on index cards. Then the school librarian can create a "staff recommendations" section in the library and display the cards and books, or she can display each card in the stacks, where the book is shelved. If the kids have questions about a book, they can ask the librarian or go directly to the staff member who recommended it.

Reading Buddies

Not all kids are going to join a book club or read a book that has been recommended by a peer or adult. For those kids, one way to ensure that literate conversations are taking place is to pair them up with reading buddies, within the same class, within the same grade, or even across different grades. As you think about pairings or groupings, keep in mind your immigrant and refugee students and their needs. There may be times that they will benefit from partnering up with one another, but they also need to have buddies who can be language models and provide them with new perspectives. Literate conversations can make a meaningful impact on all students' reading growth, and learning and reading buddies can be a fun way to facilitate those conversations.

Read-Alouds

The ideal read-aloud is interactive, meaning you don't just read the book to children. You also make time to discuss the book as you are reading it and/or after you've read it. In that sense, a read-aloud is a literate conversation in real time. Research tells us that reading aloud is critical to children's development as readers and thinkers (American Academy of Pediatrics 2014; Bernstein 2010; Cunningham & Zibulsky 2014; Mol & Bus 2011; Needlman 2014). In *The Read-Aloud Handbook,* the godfather of read-alouds, Jim Trelease, asserts that reading aloud can "condition the child's brain to associate reading with pleasure, create background knowledge, build vocabulary, and provide a reading role model" (Trelease, 2006). It's not only important in building literacy skills and a lifelong love of reading, it's fun and gives us time to bond with our children. In the Scholastic *Kids & Family Reading Report, 7th Edition* (2019), parents and children say that they love read-aloud time because "it is a special time with each other."

Read-alouds should be taking place in every classroom in America. All kids benefit from being read to, but students who are rarely read to at home, including many immigrant and refugee students, benefit the most from hearing fluent readers read and discussing the text. As a principal, I would go into classrooms and read to students often. Not only was it one of the highlights of my day, but it also sent a message to everyone that read-alouds were important.

Reading aloud to kids was one of my favorite things to do as principal.

Give Read-Alouds Online

Typically, videotaping and posting read-alouds of children's books on an online video-sharing platform such as YouTube requires securing permission from the original publisher, which can be time-consuming and costly. However, during the pandemic of 2020, many publishers loosened their policies. With access to books becoming limited for kids literally overnight, they allowed educators to read aloud their books online for a limited time. Many publishers have been gracious and kind in sharing their books with school communities. Kids and families love watching and listening to their teachers and principals read aloud to them. Trust me—they will love hearing you read *The Book With No Pictures* by B. J. Novak and *You Don't Want a Unicorn!* by Ame Dyckman! And they can watch and listen to you read the books over and over again, without you losing your voice. It's part of starting a conversation, of building a culture of literacy.

On a related note, many authors and celebrities are reading aloud online, such as Michelle and Barack Obama, as part of a movement to bring books to kids. How cool is that? Go to websites such as www.storylineonline.net to find a huge collection of popular children's books read by hugely popular and notable readers.

If you're looking for read-alouds in various languages for your emergent bilingual students, you can find many collections on publishers' YouTube channels, such as The Scholastic Storybook Treasures.

Lastly, if you can afford it, buy your favorite books to support the authors, illustrators, and publishers, and share them "live" in your classroom. Encourage your students and their families to do so, too, in support of those who give us these amazing books to share with one another!

Classes would often recommend books to other classes by sending "You've Been Booked!" cards with book suggestions for the teacher. After the read-aloud, the class that received a card would send a card suggesting a different book to another class, and so on. It was fun, engaging, and so important to emergent bilinguals who were hearing English read and spoken only at school.

Schoolwide Book of the Month

How powerful would it be to have an entire school engaged in literate conversations around one book? Now imagine if there were a different book every month with a different theme. While the depth of conversations may vary depending on the grade level, the power of everyone discussing one book—and the ideas that spring from the discussion—can be transformative for a school. For example, if your school is part of the Character Counts program and has spent time working with students on building positive schoolwide character traits, you might choose a book that connects to one of the traits. If January's character trait, for example, is "kindness," then having everyone read *Be Kind* by Pat Zietlow Miller would lead to some deep discussions throughout the school. Not only will your character-building program benefit from an exploration of a trait-related children's book, your students will also benefit from the ongoing literate conversations, as well as the social-emotional learning that will naturally occur.

Virtual Conversations

To build and sustain a culture of literacy in a school, teachers and administrators need to make sure that literate conversations are happening all of the time—whether in person, or online. There are many ways to sustain the culture of literacy that is so important in your school. For example, if members of your school community are at home for extended periods of time, ask them to take photos of themselves reading in their favorite places outside of school. In the kitchen. During a hike in the woods. At a local park. Ask them to send the photos to you and sprinkle them into your emails and newsletters to the community

at large. This serves several purposes. It reminds everyone that literacy is your focus as a school. It personalizes your messages and showcases the people in your school. And it can start those literate conversations: "What book is Bobby reading at home? I wonder if it's good. Is that the newest book by Jason Chin?"

But the conversations shouldn't stop there. Your communications should include book talks, book trailers, video links to authors, and resource pages for parents to read at home with their children. Provide a space for students and parents to give feedback, respond, and engage in the conversation.

But that's still not enough. I've seen teachers conduct small-group reading lessons on a video-conferencing platform, such as Zoom. I've seen teachers effectively watch (and rewatch) video read-alouds with kids and pause at critical moments to engage in deep discussions about the characters and

PURSUIT OF CONVERSATION

Embrace Books for Change

Project LIT Community (Libraries in the Community) is a grassroots organization founded by high school English teacher Jarred Amato and his students to bring high-quality, culturally relevant books to communities that struggle with access to books. Its main objective is to transform schools and school communities through literature. Their family literacy nights have evolved into monthly Family Book Club

Breakfasts that involve reading and talking about a book. Kids, staff members, and families show up to these morning gatherings to discuss books such as *The Hate U Give* by Angie Thomas and *All American Boys* by Jason Reynolds in hopes of not only understanding the characters better, but also understanding the world better. Today, chapters of Project LIT Community can be found in 48 states.

plot. I've seen teachers arrange virtual visits from authors of the books they are studying, with readings and rich follow-up discussions.

At Barrett Ranch, during the time of distance learning, some teachers continued their student book club meetings—on Zoom. They made sure kids had the books by dropping them off at homes, they dressed up as characters from the books during calls, and enjoyed snacks online together as they discussed the book. Building a culture of literacy requires coming up with meaningful book-related experiences for all students, whether done in person, or from a distance.

Literate Conversations at Home

So what can we do for our students when they go home? Many parents of immigrant and refugee students, like my parents when we first arrived in America, aren't able to read to their children in English. If that describes parents in your school community, encourage them to read aloud books in their home language! Let's go back to Jim Trelease and examine the benefits of reading aloud to children with an eye toward immigrant and refugee children.

Associating reading with pleasure doesn't need to happen in English. Building background knowledge doesn't either. Building vocabulary in a primary language creates a bridge to learning vocabulary in a second language (Goldenberg, 2011). And finally, a reading role model can be anyone who loves sharing a good book, regardless of the language he or she speaks. If parents aren't comfortable reading in English yet, ask them to read with their children in their home language. Not only will that engage parents in their children's learning and your school's efforts to promote literacy, it also sends an inclusive message that you honor and respect all members of your school community.

In our school, we established a parent resource center that included many children's books in several of the languages spoken by our students and their families, including Russian, Ukrainian, and Spanish. We purchased the books from online publishers and retailers specializing in multilingual books. We also helped parents understand how to read aloud to their kids—letting them know it is okay to stop and ask questions and have discussions while reading. It's important to keep in mind that many recent immigrant and refugee families may not have the financial resources to purchase books for their children. Therefore, allow families to borrow the books. Where can you find the funds? Again, it's a matter of prioritizing the effort and valuing it.

When I was young, there were very few children's books written in Vietnamese, my home language. A few decades later, when I was a classroom teacher, there was more than a handful of bilingual books in the home languages of my English learners. Today, you can easily find online translations of some of the most popular children's books. (*Harry Potter and the Sorcerer's Stone*, for example, has been translated into over 76 languages!) Think about a family that arrived in America from their war-torn country. Members of that

family are building a new life in hopes of a better future. They are learning the language and culture. Now, imagine lending a copy of *Dreamers* by Yuyi Morales, translated into their home language, for them to read aloud as a family in the evening. As they read and talk about that migrant story, and the gifts the characters bring with them from their home countries, consider the impact on the child and his or her family. I wish Morales's book had been available to me and my family decades ago because it would have made a huge difference in our lives. Through the power of the read-aloud, we can all make a difference in the lives of immigrants and refugees in our school communities.

We Need to Talk

Yes, let's talk. Literate conversations about books not only engage students in reading, but facilitate their academic and social-emotional growth. You can find time for students to have those conversations in a variety of fun and engaging ways. Literate conversations for immigrant and refugee students provide a natural and less threatening path to academic, language, and cultural learning. Whether they join a book club or offer a book talk, the conversations that follow will make a lasting impression on them.

(L) Posing on a $500 Cadillac: Vy, myself, James, and my dad (from left to right).

(R) One of my first school photos—bowl cuts were in style back then.

AN EDUCATION

ONE BULLET TO HIS HEAD DIDN'T END THE NIGHTMARE. Yes, the mass murderer committed suicide with a single shot after spraying children and their teachers with countless rounds of lead and hate. Although he is dead, the nightmare lives on.

The shooting at the Sandy Hook Elementary School in Newtown, Connecticut, took place in 2012. Twenty children and six adults were murdered, making it the deadliest school shooting in our country's history. For many of us in America, in education, it is seared into our personal and collective memories. How do we stop this horror from happening again? How do we assure parents that their children are safe in our schools? It could happen to any of us, at any time.

Almost two decades before the Sandy Hook massacre, in 1989, a similar incident occurred at Cleveland Elementary School in Stockton, California. A lone gunman entered the playground amid the tetherball and kickball games and used his semi-automatic assault weapon to murder five children and one teacher, while wounding over 30 others. All five children killed were under 10 years old and either Cambodian or Vietnamese Americans. In fact, most of the students at the campus were immigrants or refugees from Southeast Asia. In a newspaper interview following the incident, a former coworker of the gunman said that he had a seething hatred for Vietnamese immigrants and blamed us for taking jobs meant for white Americans. I was in high school at the time but my youngest siblings were about the same age as the victims. Our schools were about 30 minutes from Cleveland Elementary School, and I remember being frightened that we were next. I'm sure my parents felt the same, but we never talked about our fears. We just wanted to go to school every day, learn, and safely return home after school to be together as a family. We just wanted, in a word, an education. Just like those kids in Stockton. Just like those kids in Newtown. On top of that, the shooting in Stockton heightened my awareness that I was an immigrant, an outsider, but it wasn't the first time.

Almost everything about my family immigration story—fleeing Saigon, arriving at Camp Pendleton, adjusting to life in America, and struggling to make ends meet—I don't remember. I wish I did, but I think, at three years old, I was just too young. My cousin, Vy, who is four years older, has faint recollections. He was with us as we fled Saigon that fateful day and he lived with us in America until the day he left for college. I consider him more an older brother than cousin.

I always felt a little bad for Vy because he was always the first to jump into the fire for us. For example, he was the first to go to school in America. On his first day of school, my parents dressed him in donated clothes—a combination of a girl's blouse, way-too-tight jeans, and yellow rain boots. He probably thought he looked dashing. Rain boots were new to us, and my parents had mistakenly thought they were more

Life, Literacy, and the Pursuit of Happiness

formal than footwear that was familiar to us: flip-flops. Vy was the first to participate in school activities. I remember watching him run in a track meet after school, but not from the bleachers. We watched from outside the fence because my parents weren't sure if there was an admissions charge. Vy ended up liking school, making friends, and doing well academically, so by the time I first stepped into a classroom, I thought I was ready.

School was where I first fully realized that I was an immigrant. Being the only Asian American kid in my classrooms all the way up to middle school, I was frequently asked if I was Chinese and if I knew Kung Fu. While I made friends, I was constantly reminded that I was different. I looked different from the other kids. I ate different things. I spoke a different language at home, and lived with my extended family. As such, I found myself yo-yoing between two cultures, wanting to be accepted and loved in both.

Learning at school came pretty easy to me, though. Early on, I was pulled out with a few Mexican American kids, who were probably from migrant families that were working farms in the Valley, to get much-needed help in learning English. I didn't like being pulled out of class, but I now appreciate the fact that the staff used resources to help us learn English. After a few years, I didn't need any more ESL instruction because I pretty much became fluent.

That said, during my senior year in high school, I was pulled out of class one last time for a final ESL exam. I had just been accepted to the University of California at Berkeley and was given the exam. I remember the essay question asking me to write about what was happening in a drawing of a boy climbing a tree to retrieve a cat. I filled five pages in the test booklet to make sure that those in charge knew I was ready for Berkeley.

Contrary to the stereotype of Asians as "tiger parents," my mom and dad never involved themselves too much in my schooling, unless you count when they told me they wanted me to become a doctor (a medical one, not a "fake" one with a doctorate!). Otherwise, it was pretty much academic laissez-faire in my house. A part of that was probably due to the fact that I was a pretty good student and they didn't have to worry too much about my ability to keep up.

And while we're on the subject of stereotypes, I never took piano lessons—in fact, I had to beg my parents to rent me a trumpet so I could play in the school band. They never said to me, "You need to get into a great college, so prepare for those SAT exams," or "You should have taken more AP classes." It took me a while to understand why they didn't pressure me. But it finally dawned on me: My parents didn't really know what school was about, even in Vietnam. You see, in Vietnam, to get into high school, you had to have money or top test scores in your class. They had neither. While my mom was able to convince her parents to send her to school through eighth grade, she reluctantly dropped out because of the financial hardship. My dad never went to high school in Vietnam because he needed to work to help his parents. While they remain two of the smartest people I know, they just didn't have the opportunity of a formal education.

Now put into the mix the idea of school in another country, in another language. My mom later said, "My hope, my dream, was for all of my children to become educated—to have something that I was never able to get. We could teach you how to be a good person of character at home. That was our job. But, we trusted the school to teach you what we couldn't."

Every refugee and immigrant has a story, and while it may be tempting to lump them all into the same group, it can lead to misunderstanding and hinder our efforts to help. A refugee from war-torn Syria will have different experiences from an immigrant from Taiwan on a work visa. When you truly understand where people come from, where they are now, and where they want to go in terms of their hopes and dreams, you will have a better sense of how to serve them and their children. Some immigrant families come to America with education and skills that will take them far. But there are many who have neither of those advantages and must start from nothing. My parents, like many refugee and immigrant parents, had no choice but to trust schools with their children and their children's futures. They had no idea how to navigate the school system, and it wasn't just because of the language barrier. As good educators, we have to earn immigrant and refugee children's trust every day and work to ensure that they find success in school and beyond.

Life, Literacy, and the Pursuit of Happiness

COLLECTION

"Make it a rule never to give a child a book you would not read yourself."
—GEORGE BERNARD SHAW

El Castillo is a project by Mexican artist Jorge Méndez Blake. It is a brick wall—literally—that measures 75 feet long by 13 feet tall, and is made up of thousands of red bricks. It was first installed in 2007 at the José Cornejo Franco Public Library in Guadalajara, the artist's hometown. It would be a perfectly symmetrical brick wall if it were not for one book wedged into its foundation— a copy of *El Castillo* (*The Castle*) by Franz Kafka. This one book, measuring only about an inch, distorts the entire wall above it. You can't look at the huge wall without noticing the ripple effect that one tiny book causes. It's an amazing sight and important reminder of the power of one book in the lives of our students.

El Castillo by Jorge Méndez Blake artfully shows the difference that one book can make.

Of course, it has to be the right book. What book turned you into a reader? *The Catcher in the Rye* had a significant impact on me as a kid—I had never met anyone like Holden Caulfield, but got to know him like a best friend, thanks to J. D. Salinger's flawless writing. Books and stories can make a difference.

The National Council for Teachers of English (NCTE) recently launched an initiative called Build Your Stack, designed to help teachers build their knowledge of books and, by extension, their classroom libraries. This goes along with the Council's belief that "the right book in the right hands can transform a life."

So what is the right book for each of your students? Well, it depends on the kid. Some kids will want "mirrors," books in which they see themselves, while some kids need "doors" to escape into a different world. Some kids have a huge appetite for reading about their interests and passions, while others will want to explore the unknown. Some kids will stick with a certain genre, while others are fascinated to try out different ones. It depends on the kid. Not all Black boys will be interested in reading *Long Way Down* by Jason Reynolds. Not all Asian girls will be interested in reading *A Single Shard* by Linda Sue Park. And that is why student choice is so important.

The Freedom to Choose Any Book

Students become better readers and are more likely to develop lifelong reading skills when we allow them to choose what they read. That makes sense, right? You read more of what you are interested in reading. Yes, you'll read what you're required to read, but you won't read any more than you have to. This not only makes practical sense, but is also supported by research. According to Guthrie and Humenick (2004), self-selected reading is twice as effective as teacher-selected reading in engaging readers and building comprehension. Allington and Gabriel (2012) concluded, "The research on student-selected reading is robust and conclusive. Students read more, understand more, and are more likely to continue reading when they have the opportunity to choose what they read." When kids are given a choice in what they read, they are more motivated to read (Gallagher, 2009; Pruzinsky, 2014; Sewell, 2003).

To create an environment that engages all students in reading, we must provide them with daily opportunities for choice in what they read. That does not mean they shouldn't be expected to read books or stories that they don't want to read. There are times in school (as well as in life) when one must read something that he or she doesn't want to read. Who, for example, wants to read the instruction manual to a new air conditioner? But when it's 108 degrees outside, and you're sweating through your clothes, you're going to have to do some unpleasant reading. However, it is clear, if we want all our students, including our immigrant and refugee students, to develop a lifelong love of reading, we must give them the freedom to choose what they read as often as we can.

The Importance of Many Books

If you're like me, you love browsing the aisles of bookstores. I just love the variety of books available—the different authors, genres, and topics. I love to see what's new. Now imagine if every time you walked into your favorite bookstore, you saw the same old books on the shelves. Imagine if that bookstore carried only a small number of books with little variety. You won't find Kate DiCamillo's latest release...or the newest Dog Man...or that hot-off-the-press biography of basketball star Michael Jordan. How uninspiring would that bookstore be for you? It probably wouldn't be your favorite bookstore any longer. How motivated would you be to pick up a book and read? It's the same for kids in school.

If we want students to read more, we need to provide them with a wide variety of engaging books in many genres. According to Robert Marzano (2004), a successful reading program provides a wealth of books and other reading materials to students in every grade. They are essential to building students' background knowledge and increasing their vocabulary and comprehension. The research supports that fact. Student access to interesting texts produced reading achievement about four times as much as systematic phonics instruction (Guthrie & Humenick, 2004).

Where can they find those texts on campus? School and classroom libraries. Students who have access to well-designed school and classroom libraries interact more with books, spend more time reading, have more positive attitudes toward reading, and have higher levels of reading achievement (2005 NAEP Report).

Book access for children of low-income backgrounds is especially critical because their families typically don't have the financial resources to buy books. In addition, they have limited resources to provide their children with experiences to build background knowledge, so improving book access can help build background knowledge for these children. Researchers Neuman and Celano (2012) found that the most successful way to improve reading achievement of children from low-income backgrounds is to increase their access to print.

Students who have access to print in their classrooms and schools have the opportunity to read more, and research says they do, in fact, read more. Because students from low-income backgrounds have access to many fewer books than their counterparts from high-income backgrounds (Neuman & Celano, 2001; 2012), providing more books to students in our most under-resourced communities can help close the opportunity gap between all students.

The culture of any community can be partly defined by the literature found in that community. Therefore, to build a thriving culture of literacy for all, your collection of books must be dynamic and engaging. It must be updated constantly to reflect stories from around the world, as well as stories from within the community.

Building Our Stacks at School

If book access is a key to student achievement and its impact is more pronounced in low-income communities, then it should be our top priority, as educators, to get more books. Of course, we'll want to get the newest books, the most relevant and interesting ones to students, and ones that will serve as windows and mirrors for all our students. This is what is commonly referred to as a "no-brainer."

But wait, what? Did I hear someone say something about money? You don't have the money to buy more books for your schools? Take it from someone who's been in schools for a while now: There's always money. Yes, I said it and I'll say it a little louder. There is always money. It's just a matter prioritizing—specifically, of finding money and, if necessary, reallocating it. As Richard Allington astutely points out, "Strangely, there is always money available for workbooks, photocopying, and computers; yet many schools claim that they have no budget for large, multileveled classroom libraries" (Allington & Gabriel, 2012).

A few years ago, I decided as principal to prioritize what the research clearly tells us and provide kids with access to engaging books. Every classroom teacher received $500 to buy books for his or her classroom library at the beginning of the year. The deal was, they couldn't buy whatever books they wanted. They needed to buy books that their students wanted—ones that reflected their interests and backgrounds. The teachers and I came up with an interest inventory and used it to survey kids about their favorite genres, authors, and topics. Not only did we start building our classroom libraries and making more books available to kids, we also got to know our students better. We got to know their passions, hobbies, backgrounds, and interests. I asked teachers to read up on the importance of using books as windows and mirrors. And we bought books. In

Ensuring that our classroom libraries were stocked with the best children's books available.

our efforts to stock up our libraries, we researched and explored book lists and recommendations and became immersed in the world of children's literature. We bought lots of books. Each book was stamped on the inside cover with these words: "Barrett Ranch Classroom Library: 'One child, one teacher, one book, and one pen can change the world.'—Malala Yousafzai." We've funded classroom libraries every year since.

Carry-Over Money

I know your next question. How do we fund this effort every year? Barrett Ranch has about 24 classrooms and, if I'm doing my math correctly, the bill comes out to be $12,000 per year. Again, the answer is prioritizing. We immediately deprioritized things that we normally would fund—software and technology that would need to be updated later anyway, travel and conferences, etc. I say "deprioritize" because we didn't take those line items off of the books; we just waited to see if there was extra money toward the budget year's end. And I'll say this out loud: There's always extra money toward the budget year's end. Of course, you have to budget for unforeseen expenses every year. You also don't ever spend all the money that you've

Fund Classroom Libraries

Use these reflection questions as starting points for discussions with your team as you work together to build your classroom libraries. You may start by organizing staff members into small groups and then share out to the whole group.

- What are some of the things that you can deprioritize at your school?
- What interests your students? What types of books do you think they would find engaging? What types of books can be windows and mirrors for them?

It's always important to stay current and knowledgeable about children's literature. Here are some ways to do that:

- Go to the local library or bookstore and just browse the new releases.
- Attend a book festival as a professional development opportunity. Teachers and staff members can meet authors of children's books, learn about new books, and possibly bring new teaching ideas back to the school and district.
- Explore lists of diverse books, award winners, and recommendations from reliable sources. See Dr. Vu's Hot Reads at the back of the book, or go to scholastic.com/LifeLiteracyResources for a greater list of resources.

budgeted. Usually, there's money left over. It's called "carry-over" money. And that money can be used to fund the other things that aren't as important as books.

Indian Prairie School District in Illinois took this idea a step further. A district committee called the Volume Reading Committee was charged with increasing student reading. One of the first action items was funding classroom libraries. Rhonda Jenkins, committee member and the district's Library Media Center Director, says, "Funding teachers' classroom libraries was on the top of our action list. Teachers should not have to pay for their classroom books!" The committee convinced the district to use the millions of dollars they saved from transitioning from traditional textbooks to less expensive digital books to fund the district's classroom libraries. Every elementary teacher in all 21 schools received $250 to spend at a Scholastic Book Fair at the beginning of the school year. What a great way to start off the year! And, get this, they did it again later that year at a Spring Book Fair!

Grants, Donations, and Collaborations

There are other ways to obtain books for classroom and school libraries that don't require much money, but they do require creativity and collaboration. First, you can always go the route of asking for the money through writing grants or requesting donations. A simple online search will yield results, such as the organization We Need Diverse Books, whose mission is to arrange for book donations to schools (as well as work with publishers to ensure underrepresented stories are told). And there's always DonorsChoose to give your classroom libraries a boost.

Another option is to collaborate with outside organizations to share resources. For example, you can work with a local library to have a bookmobile come to your school regularly to make new books available to students. Not only is this a no-cost way to get books into kids' hands, it increases the library's circulation and reach in the community.

There are many community organizations that collect used books and donate them to classrooms. A 2018 Exemplary Reading Program School, Palmer Elementary School in Chicago, is known for its extensive classroom libraries. Principal Jennifer Dixon says, "There are books everywhere. We don't have a school library, so all of our books are in the classrooms." Most of those books have been donated by a community organization called BooksFirst! Chicago. Principal Dixon says, "It's pretty much a group of parent volunteers who collect donated children's books to bring to Chicago schools. They store them in their basements and homes, organize them, box them up, and drive them over to the schools in their station wagons. It's pretty amazing." Considering that 50 percent of all Chicago Public Schools don't have a school library, this work, which is carried out by parent volunteers, is critical in ensuring access to books for all kids. If your school community doesn't have BooksFirst! or something like it, have your parent organization start one up!

With all of this knowledge on the importance of school libraries, classroom libraries, and surrounding our kids with books at school, most of us would consider it educational malpractice if one advocated for closing a library to create a makerspace or computer lab. While these spaces can be valuable learning resources for students, they should not be created at the expense of a library. Cutting funds for books or laying off a school librarian is a similar dereliction of duty, as far as I'm concerned.

Getting Books Into Homes

Okay, now that we've established the need for books in schools, how about books at home? Longitudinal studies involving hundreds of thousands of children show the same findings: When children are raised in homes with even just 25 books, they will stay in school significantly longer than those students who don't have any books in the home (Evans et al., 2010; Mullis & Martin, 2007). In a large study involving nearly 100,000 American children, researchers found that the one variable that correlated significantly to reading achievement was the number of books in the home (McQuillan, 1998).

How can you help families build a collection of books at home? Start by letting them know the huge impact. Without being too verbose, put some of the research in your newsletter or send out an email message right before your school's book fair to encourage parents to buy books for their children.

From there, direct families to sources for books—the local library, bookstore, or online libraries and stores. Districts, especially ones that have invested in 1:1 technology, should look at digital book lending programs such as Hoopla, Libby, or Epic! to provide students and teachers access to books. Students can access hundreds of books from home, which include graphic novels, bestsellers, and new releases, many of which are available in languages other than English.

And most important, make sure your families know how to connect to these programs! I'm speaking from experience as a parent, when I was told during Back to School Night that students had access to ebooks through a school subscription. But we parents never got information on how to access the subscription, and it was never mentioned again that year!

At most public libraries, you'll find a used-books-for-sale section. This is a great resource for parents who are interested in building a home library for their children. Encourage parents who don't speak English to buy or borrow books in their primary language, and read them to their children. Nowadays, many books are translated into many languages, especially bestsellers, and they are available online or at your public library. If our goal is to engage students and instill in them the joy of reading for a lifetime, it doesn't matter in what language parents are reading.

When former student Michael Duran proposed creating a Little Free Library for our school for an Eagle Scout project, I asked him to make three for different areas of the school. He thought about it—probably hesitant to triple his work—and agreed. He worked with our district facilities team to install the libraries, which house hundreds of books for students and parents to take and share. Does taking one book from the Little Free Library make a difference in building a child's stack at home? It's only one book, but in some cases, it may be the first book a child owns. In other cases, it may ignite a personal desire to own and collect more books. The book may be just the book for the child to start building his or her stack.

Michael made three of these little libraries for the school. We eventually painted them with different book themes.

Help Students Build Their Own Stacks

Principal Todd Nesloney and his team at Webb Elementary School in Navasota, Texas, decided to help all of their students build their own stacks. The school has about 775 students, 90 percent of whom are receiving free and reduced-price lunches, and many of whom do not have home libraries. They made independent reading a priority and used Title I funds to buy books for kids. They collaborated with Scholastic Book Fairs to host a Buy One, Get One (BOGO) event, at which all students were given $100 to purchase any books they wanted. With the BOGO deal, they each actually got $200 worth of books. Imagine a family of three kids with $600 worth of books in their home, creating, in essence, a home library! Needless to say, the BOGO event was a big success for the school and the families. According to Principal Nesloney, "To say this event was life-changing would be an understatement. The excitement from the children, as well as the countless tears that were shed from the opportunity for many to pick a book to own for the first time in their life, was an experience I will never forget. Over the next year, we watched reading scores increase, but we watched a love of reading bloom even more."

A Library for Everyone: Exploring Windows and Mirrors

One of my former teachers, Jennifer DeBortoli, gave me a copy of the picture book *A Different Pond* by Bao Phi. She left it on my desk with a note that said, "Don—I think you'll like this book." She was wrong. I loved this book.

A Different Pond is a story about a young Vietnamese American boy who wakes up in the wee hours of the morning to go fishing with his dad. They go early because his dad has a second job he must be at later that morning. They

fish because, "Everything in America costs a lot of money" and they are recent refugees. They fish, not for fun but for survival. From there, already looking exhausted, mom and dad both head off to work, leaving the kids to take care of one another. The book depicts a family working together lovingly to make ends meet. At dinnertime, parents and children reunite and gather around the table. They tell funny stories, talk about their day, discuss homework, and eat some rice and fish.

When I was a child in school, I would've loved to have had books like *A Different Pond*—in other words, stories about other Vietnamese people. To be honest, I would've loved to have had any book even remotely representing any Asian American experience. The only time during school we read about Asians or Asian Americans was during social studies, when we learned about World War II and the Japanese Internment. The reading usually consisted of a page or two in a textbook and certainly didn't celebrate my culture or history. Far too often, we neglect to tell the stories of the people who make up our schools and communities. And, as a result, we send a message that they are not important, that they live in the mainstream's margins, that their story is not worth being told.

After reading *A Different Pond*, it took me a while to process what this story meant to me as a reader, a Vietnamese American reader. I connected with the characters in ways that I'm not sure I can explain, but here's my shot at it.

I knew exactly how the boy felt waking up early, excited to spend some time with his father and hopeful about contributing food to the dinner table. I remember fishing with my family. I remember the red and white floaters and the excitement of catching a fish. I associate those times more with joy than struggle. *A Different Pond* reminded me that my story is forever woven together with my parents'. It led me to reflect on their refugee experience—a journey to a new and unknown country to escape war and persecution. I can't imagine their fear, but marvel at their courage to learn a new language and embrace a new culture. I look at family pictures during our first few years in America and, in them, can see the exhausted looks on the faces of my mom and dad. The beautiful illustrations from *A Different Pond* (Thi Bui is the book's amazing illustrator) reminded me of those pictures. The bags under the eyes of the mom and dad in the book represent so much more to me, one who has experienced the characters' experience, than just exhaustion. They also represent sacrifice, perseverance, and hope for a brighter future.

If you have a hard time understanding my perspective (because you likely don't share my history and background), indulge me a bit and imagine yourself taking your family away to live in a country that is very different from America. You live in that country for decades and your kids go to school there. They learn the country's dominant language and adopt its culture. You are a citizen of this new country now but you still have your American roots. You look different from most of the people who were born there and, in some ways, you are different. For the most part, life is good, except there are no books or stories about Americans who live in your new country. There are no Thanksgivings, Fourth of Julys, and other holidays and celebrations from your past (or present). No stories that include people who look like you or share your experiences. Would that make you feel less important in your new country?

Far too often, we neglect to tell the stories of the people who make up our schools and communities. And, as a result, we send a message that they are not important, that they live in the mainstream's margins, that their story is not worth being told.

Colin Huynh, one of the few Vietnamese American students in Ms. DeBortoli's class, said to her after reading *A Different Pond*, "I can't believe they said Vietnam. That's where my family came from. I just loved it." Decades later, my family and I are still looking to see ourselves represented in American culture—to see ourselves in the stories that make our country great.

Colin and I started our own book club after bonding over Bao Phi's *A Different Pond*.

This is why diverse books are important—not only because they make us feel important, but also because they make us important. How powerful is the need to see yourself in the stories that you read? Jason Reynolds, *New York Times* bestselling author of young adult books and one of *Time* magazine's 2019 Next 100 Changemakers, says that he didn't read a book from cover to cover until he was 17. In an interview with Gayle King, he explains, "It wasn't about the actual reading process. It was about the fact that I didn't think that stories were written for me" (Reynolds, 2017). He says that when he and his classmates were assigned *Moby Dick*, he didn't rise to the challenge because he and many of his friends had never seen a whale or a boat in real life before. The story had no relevance in his life. He couldn't relate to it. He was looking for stories that meant something to him—ones in which he would see himself, his life. And when he started to see himself and his community in poetry, books, and music, he began to dedicate his life to amplifying that singular idea that literacy can change lives if books could serve as mirrors and windows for all young people. Do the right books make a difference in the world? Imagine if Jason Reynolds were never assigned another book to read after *Moby Dick*.

PART III
PURSUIT OF HAPPINESS

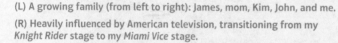

(L) A growing family (from left to right): James, mom, Kim, John, and me.

(R) Heavily influenced by American television, transitioning from my *Knight Rider* stage to my *Miami Vice* stage.

THE AUDACITY OF EQUALITY

DON IS MY FIRST NAME, BUT IT REALLY WASN'T MY first name. My parents named me Hùng, which means "heroic" in Vietnamese. With the accent mark, it's pronounced with a downward inflection and sounds almost like the word *whom*. I'm pretty sure my parents didn't name me Hùng, hoping that I'd someday live up to its definition. Instead, they just chose a popular name for boys in Vietnam. In America? Not so much. I felt like I was constantly explaining to others how to correctly pronounce my name. Like many kids with uncommon names, I hated those days when the teacher was out and the substitute took attendance out loud. Inevitably, she or he would get to the end of the alphabetical list, pause with a confused expression, and say, "Hung? Who? Mr. Vu?" I hated it, but didn't blame substitutes for not knowing how to pronounce my name correctly. What I hated most was when kids made fun of my name. That hurt, and it happened often at school.

All that is to say, after my parents eventually became naturalized American citizens, they asked us kids if we wanted to pick "American" names. I'm not proud of my decision. I desperately wanted to change my name for several reasons. I wanted to fit in. I was the only Asian American kid in my class and, at times, felt like I didn't belong.

Did I say I wanted to fit in? This was in the mid-80s, and I was a big fan of the show *Miami Vice*. I went through a period of wearing fluorescent-colored shirts, baggy light-colored pants, dark shades, and no socks, like the characters on the show. I listened to the *Miami Vice* soundtrack on my cassette tape player. (If you're a young educator, you can google "cassette tape player"!) I wanted to be Sonny Crockett—the cool-as-a-cucumber detective played by the great actor Don Johnson. Okay, you can figure out the rest of the story. "Sonny Vu" wasn't going to fly at school, but "Don Vu" would. It had a nice ring to it. My little brother was a fan of the Bond spy movies and wanted to be 007—thus, "James Vu" was born. My cousin Vy was a big fan of martial arts and martial-arts movies (we all were) and named himself after the master himself, Bruce Lee. For better or worse, you can see the enormous impact television and movies had on us young refugees back then.

While I ended up losing part of my identity, losing my birth name was not too traumatic. But for the immigrant or refugee student who bravely retains the name he or she was given at birth, their name is one of the first things in their identity that is assaulted. I'm not talking about a teacher mispronouncing the name—that is understandable and forgivable. What is not forgivable are the deliberate attempts to marginalize and humiliate someone because of their name. In 2020, at Laney College in Oakland, California, a couple of miles from the very diverse community where I lived and taught, a math professor asked a Vietnamese American student if she would "anglicize" her name. In an email to her, he explained that her name, Phuc Bui Nguyen, sounded too much like an "insult in English." When she told him she was offended by his suggestion, he doubled down and wrote to her, "Your name sounds like 'F-ck Boy.' If I lived in Vietnam and my name sounded like 'Eat a D-ck,' I would change it to avoid embarrassing myself and the people who have to say it. I understand you are offended, but you need to understand your name is offensive-sounding in my language. I repeat my request." Phuc Bui did not change her name, and the professor was placed on administrative leave. This is just one example of how racism and xenophobia can seep into our classrooms and assault our immigrant and refugee students.

Incredibly, that incident happened in 2020, at a college where 80 percent of the students are students of color. The identities of immigrants and refugees are attacked every day, and their names are just one of the casualties. Kelly Yang, author of *Front Desk, The Three Keys,* and *Parachutes,* recalls that her elementary school teacher said that her Chinese name was a joke and took it upon herself to name her after a blonde character on the television show *Beverly Hills 90210.*

No matter how successful you are in American society, you and your name can still be a target. Vice President Kamala Harris's first name was consistently mispronounced and mocked by several prominent opposing politicians during the 2020 Presidential campaign. Each and every time they attacked her name, they sent the message that if you have a name like Kamala, you are not as American as if your name was, say, Karen. Those politicians may deny what I'm saying, but there's no other way to interpret their racist and bullying behavior.

When I meet Americans today with names such as Dalopo, Việt, Aashritha, and Tuấn, I am so happy that they didn't feel the need to change them to fit in. In a way, they are saying, "My name is as American as yours, and you'll just need to learn how to pronounce it correctly."

As a kid growing up in the '80s and '90s, I always struggled to balance the culture of my family and the culture of America at the same time. I was constantly caught between two worlds, and it was especially apparent at school. I didn't want to be seen as different from my friends and classmates—most of whom were white, middle-class kids. It was always awkward at the beginning of the school year when I would have to inevitably explain to the teacher how to pronounce my name. I remember

Life, Literacy, and the Pursuit of Happiness

one year, in fact, when the teacher actually made fun of it—causing an uproar of laughter in the classroom. It was painful at times when kids at school would call me a "chink" or "gook," tell me "go back to your country," and make fun of Asians using what they considered an Asian accent. I never reported those incidents, and most of your students will probably never report incidents like these to you.

At home, I remember hiding the rice cooker and speaking only English to my parents whenever my friends would come over after school. I just wanted to fit in. Luckily, my parents and grandparents were proud people who never let me forget where I came from. They found ways for us to engage in the Vietnamese community one city over—at church functions, cultural celebrations, and community and family gatherings. Vietnamese was the primary language in our home, and we kids would be reprimanded if we were caught speaking English to one another. Most of the time, we lived like Vietnamese refugees sheltering in place in America. I never went to a movie theater with my family growing up. We didn't eat at restaurants. I do remember doing some distinctly "American" things, such as going to an amusement park, watching a drive-in movie, taking road trips to visit family in Southern California, and, on special occasions, having hamburgers and fries for dinner. The funny thing is, I never felt I lacked anything growing up. I just understood early on that my family experiences were much different from those of my friends.

Hasan Minhaj, comedian and political commentator, recalls in his comedy special *Homecoming King* a hate crime that he and his family experienced, just after the 9/11 terrorist attacks. After the windows of their parked car were smashed in the middle of the night, he and his dad ran out to the front of the house to survey the damage. His dad immediately began sweeping up the glass and conceded that this was a new reality for all Muslim Americans and that they had to accept it. For Minhaj's dad and so many other immigrants of his generation, there is an "immigrant tax" to pay for living in America. If you weren't born here but want to benefit from everything America has to offer, you'll have to bow your head and accept certain things in your life, such as racism and inequality. In their minds, there's always a trade-off, a price to pay. Living in America meant you will always be a second-class citizen.

Hasan, on the other hand, was enraged by being a victim of a hate crime. Acting as if he had a copy of the Declaration of Independence in his hands, he remembered thinking, "Nah, I'm in Honors Gov. I have it right here. Life, liberty, and the pursuit of happiness. All men are created equal. It says it right here. I'm equal." He later says, "I was born here, so I actually have the audacity of equality" (Storer, 2017).

I didn't really understand the audacity of equality until after I left my home for college. Berkeley, California, was a different world from the one I grew up in—it was a different version of America. My world was no longer homogenous and white. I was now surrounded by people from all walks of life, and being different was valued and even celebrated. It was a transformative experience that caused a paradigm shift in me that carries on today.

While at Berkeley, I began to realize that being American wasn't about how you dress, what you eat, or what language you speak. It wasn't about who you love, where you come from, or what political party you belong to. It was about something much more. I realized that being American is about acknowledging that you are truly equal in this country, no matter who you are. You can't be fully American if you have to hide the food you eat at home or fear to speak your home language in front of others. You can't be fully American if you don't have the same rights as the white, middle-class majority. But this audacity of equality has to be realized before you can be fully American.

Some of my friends and colleagues never had to think about all this because being American and being equal had never been an issue for them. No one had ever questioned their status or rights. No one had ever questioned any part of their identity. They were born with the expectation of equality. For refugees and immigrants, though, that isn't the case.

So now, more than ever, it is critical for us, as educators, to help immigrant and refugee students to embrace the audacity of equality. Through literacy, we can help them understand that differences are meant to be celebrated and make the world a much better place. Through literacy, we can help them realize that their stories are important and worthy of being told. And through literacy, we can help our students live full lives in pursuit of happiness.

Life, Literacy, and the Pursuit of Happiness

CONNECTION

"You think your pain and your heartbreak are unprecedented in the history of the world, but then you read. It was books that taught me that the things that tormented me most were the very things that connected me with all the people who were alive, who had ever been alive."

—JAMES BALDWIN

Books and stories not only entertain and educate us, but also connect us to the world. They also connect us to ourselves and help us embrace the audacity of equality. For a young immigrant student whose name has been questioned or mocked, reading the picture book *Alma and How She Got Her Name* by Juana Martinez-Neal may help her realize that every name is a gift of love and hope, and should be respected and honored. For any student who wants to understand what it feels like to be a Vietnamese refugee, reading *Inside Out & Back Again* by Thanhha Lai will give them a glimpse of the joy and struggles of losing one's country and finding one's identity in a new one. Literacy can change our perspectives. It can change our lives and, if we work hard enough and persevere, it can change our world. That is its power.

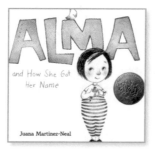

Beyond Windows and Mirrors

There are many great resources to help you find books that can be windows and mirrors for students. As I pointed out in Chapter 8, there are lots of ways to generate diverse book collections full of worthy books to share with students. But what do you do once you get those books into your schools and classrooms? What are the best strategies to use when you hold up a mirror for a child to see a clear reflection of him- or herself—or a window to see beyond him- or herself? How can you use books and stories to help support and build children's audacity of equality? What can you do to help all kids see and value diversity in the world and develop a sense of empathy for others? While it's important to provide access to books, it's just as important to know what to do with them.

Examining One's Own Perspectives

Is a story a window or a mirror? Or both? That depends on the reader, of course. It's important to discuss that question as a classroom community

so students can find meaning in their own perspectives and the perspectives of others. When reading R. J. Palacio's *Wonder*, for example, students may find themselves identifying with the lonely new kid who looks so different from his classmates. Later in the same story, they may empathize with the sibling who has been ignored and neglected at home. This kind of reflection may not come naturally for students. But you can help them by providing a safe space for them to share so that they know their contributions are respected and valued. You will also need to think about questions to ask and model think-aloud strategies during group reading.

Connecting to Other Perspectives

We want kids to see the world from perspectives other than their own, too— to walk in someone else's shoes. What better way to do that than by having students ask themselves, "How would I feel if I were that person?" or "What would I do if I were in that person's situation?"

Aspire to a New Learning Standard

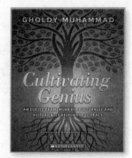

In *Cultivating Genius: An Equity Framework for Culturally and Historically Responsive Literacy,* Dr. Gholdy Muhammad (2020) presents a literacy framework that promotes four learning pursuits: identity, skills, intellect, and criticality. A focus on these new "standards" can help kids, especially those who are traditionally underserved, develop a strong sense of themselves and the world. Muhammad's pursuit of identity, in particular, invites kids to reflect on their own identities as they explore literature. It enables them to make sense of their values and beliefs. For example, when reading Jacqueline Woodson's *The Day You Begin*, students can reflect on the qualities that make them unique and the gifts they bring to their school. Her approach allows all students to connect on a profound level with the literature they are reading.

To make a literature connection, choose a well-known story, such as *The Wonderful Wizard of Oz* by L. Frank Baum, and find a version that tells the story from a different perspective, such as *Wicked* by Gregory Maguire. While *Wicked* may not be appropriate for all children, you can explain that the novel tells the story of how the Wicked Witch of the West came to be in the Land of Oz. In the end, we sympathize with the green-skinned Elphaba, understand her plight, and hope for her redemption. There are many books that tell well-known tales from different perspectives and allow students to engage in conversations about "the other side of the story." *The True Story of the Three Little Pigs* by Jon Scieszka is an especially engaging one for kids, I've found.

We want kids to see the world from perspectives other than their own, too— to walk in someone else's shoes.

Activities such as journaling from a character's perspective can be helpful in getting students to reflect on our differences and similarities. If you're exploring the theme of sacrifice while reading Shel Silverstein's *The Giving Tree*, you could have students write letters to the tree from the old man's perspective. What would he say? What did he learn in life?

Honor Different Perspectives

Many schools are homogenous and don't have students of color or families from diverse socioeconomic backgrounds. So it is especially important to expose students at those schools to books that contain viewpoints and perspectives that may not be represented in their communities. By doing that as early as possible, we open those students to learning and growing in an increasingly diverse world. While white or Asian students may never fully understand the impact of police brutality on the Black community, they may get a sense of the impact by reading about Starr Carter and her experiences in *The Hate U Give* by Angie Thomas. While these young people may not know any survivors of the Holocaust, they may get a glimpse of the sadness and pain that Anne Frank felt by reading her diary. When we provide opportunities for all kids to experience the suffering of others, we begin to build a society that is more tolerant and accepting. So how can your classroom, school, and district build on the work of storytellers like those and change the world?

How did the tree help him? You may have students role-play different characters from a story, being careful to avoid stereotyping. Role-playing characters such as Salma and Lily from Queen Rania of Jordan's *The Sandwich Swap* can help kids develop a deeper understanding of people's differences and similarities.

Comparing and Contrasting

In *Classroom Instruction That Works*, Robert Marzano and colleagues say that identifying similarities and differences is critical to enhancing students' understanding of and ability to use knowledge (Marzano, Pickering & Pollock, 2013). That strategy can be used to help students identify what makes them similar to characters and what makes them different. Using a graphic organizer such as a Venn diagram, a student can explore ways they are similar to and different from a character, such as Harry Potter or Wilbur from *Charlotte's Web*. By doing that, students can develop a better sense of who they are and also come to understand the character at a deeper level.

Be sure to provide students with time to reflect on their learning. As a class, answer questions such as, "What did you think and how did you feel when you encountered a character who was similar to you, or when you encountered one who was very different from you?" It's also important to allow students to ask any questions that they may have. They may have strong feelings about new ideas, and it's important to debrief with them about how to move forward with empathy and kindness.

Connecting to the Unknown: Building Background Knowledge

Many of our immigrant and refugee students come to us with gaps in their knowledge because they have not been in this country their entire lives. Those gaps, of course, may be cultural—knowledge that those who were born here take for granted. For example, a Valentine's Day dance at a school can be confusing for a new immigrant from Cambodia because Valentine's Day is not celebrated in that country. There may be academic gaps as well, due to language differences and/or differences in content they learned at their former school and current school. Students who come from low-income and underserved communities experience similar gaps due to a lack of certain experiences in their daily lives. Regardless of the circumstances, those gaps need to be filled for students to find success in our schools. When they are not, the proverbial achievement gap rears its ugly head.

Without life experiences that build valuable background knowledge, students will be less likely to make connections to the things they will learn in school. My school is located about an hour and a half from the Sierra Nevada Mountains, where every winter throngs of people strap on skis and snowboards to take advantage of the snow. Despite that, many of my students have never seen snow, even though they don't live too far from the mountains. When I taught in Oakland, many of my students had never been to the beach, even though the only thing that separated them from Ocean Beach in San Francisco was the Bay Bridge. When I was a kid in Manteca, California, former home of the famous Manteca Oakwood Lake Waterslides, I went to the waterslides only once, despite our searing hot summers. In all these examples, income—or lack of it—was a significant factor in preventing participation in the activities. It's true that going to the beach doesn't cost much, but many of those kids had duties at home on the weekends, such as babysitting young family members while their parents were at work. While cultural differences can play a role, many of the inequities like this come down to socioeconomics. Some families simply don't have the resources and privileges to engage in many life-enriching endeavors. And that impacts teaching and learning. When you have a student who has never seen snow, it will be more difficult for him or her to make connections when you're teaching about Alaska's climate or reading or discussing *The Snowy Day* by Ezra Jack Keats.

So what can you do? Remember, experiences build background knowledge. You can bring the snow to them. (A teacher I know did that one year upon her return from a ski weekend with her family.) Or you can plan lots of field trips and assemblies (yes, those are still important!). Marzano (2004) talks about how virtual experiences can also build background knowledge and how reading is one of the most direct ways to generate virtual experiences and build background knowledge.

Building background knowledge improves students' reading comprehension by providing context for the story (when it comes to fiction), or information (when it comes to nonfiction).

Building background knowledge improves students' reading comprehension by providing context for the story (when it comes to fiction), or information (when it comes to nonfiction). So think about what students need to know before they read a particular book. For example, if you're going to read *Write to Me: Letters From Japanese American Children to the Librarian They Left Behind* by Cynthia Grady, be sure students have some understanding of World War II internment camps. Have you ever noticed that people who are really good at trivia games, people who have expansive banks of background knowledge, are some of the most academically proficient? They tend to understand what they read at a deep level and make connections to build upon their learning. It's important to do our best to help kids build their background knowledge.

Build Cultural Knowledge

Most of us have experienced dining in a restaurant and using our background knowledge to inform what we do. We wait to be seated, we order from a menu, and we pay for the meal after we've finished it. If the waiter is good, we might add a 20-percent tip as a gesture of appreciation. However, if we included a tip after dining in Japan, it would be considered an insult to the waiter!

Building cultural knowledge is as essential as building background knowledge in our work with immigrant and refugee students who are learning a new language and are adjusting to a new culture and society. As you help your newcomers build cultural knowledge, consider these questions:

1. What are the cultural and social differences between their home countries and America?

2. How was their schooling here different from the schooling they received in the countries they left? What were the expectations for teachers, parents, and students?

3. What are some of the possible cultural hurdles that you see as they adjust to a new life in America?

Connecting to Students' Experiences and Interests

We know that choice in what students read plays a significant role in how much they read. If we want them to read more, then we must connect our students to books and stories that will resonate with them—books and stories they *want* to read. If we are serious about helping students find their place in the world through literacy, then we need to work at getting to know our students—who they are, their life experiences, and their interests and curiosities. Some teachers use interest inventories to find out about their students and use the results to inform their thinking when purchasing books for their libraries. Thanks to technology, you can do a schoolwide interest inventory using a Google Form and disaggregated data to make decisions

Barrett Ranch Student Reading Inventory

Name_____

1) What do you like to do after school or on weekends?

2) What are you really good at?

3) What kinds of books do you prefer?
☐ Fiction (Make believe) ☐ Nonfiction (Real) ☐ No preference

4) What kinds of *fiction* books do you like? (Check all that apply)
☐ Picture books   ☐ Chapter books   ☐ Graphic Novels
☐ Poetry   ☐ Cartoons   ☐ Mystery books
☐ Funny books   ☐ Sport books   ☐ Scary books
☐ Animal books   ☐ Science Fiction ☐ Historical Fiction
☐ Fantasy   ☐ Joke books   ☐ Comics

5) What kinds of *nonfiction* books do you like? (Check all that apply)
☐ Weather   ☐ Space   ☐ Animals _____
☐ History   ☐ Biographies ☐ Other _____
☐ Plants/Flowers ☐ How to
☐ Rocks/Minerals ☐ Sports

6) Do you collect anything? ☐ Yes ☐ No
    *If so, what do you collect?*_____

7) Would you like to collect anything? ☐ Yes ☐ No
    If so, what would you like to collect? _____

A sample page from the student reading inventory that we gave to kids as we made purchases for our libraries. (Credit: Jennifer DeBortoli)

for individual classroom libraries or for the school library. You can easily find out if you should, for example, acquire more nonfiction books, series books, graphic novels, or even books on unicorns! You can easily find interest inventories online. My colleagues and I did this when we started building our classroom libraries, which enabled us to make informed decisions about purchasing the books our kids would love.

Connecting to the World

Always be on the lookout for ways to connect what students are reading and learning to the real world. Not only will you pique student interests, you will also help them build and extend background knowledge. Can you bring in someone from the community who can speak to the experiences of a character in a book? If you're reading *Last Stop on Market Street* by Matt de la Peña, for example, a person who volunteers in a soup kitchen can provide a window for kids who wonder what it would be like to do that kind of work—and a mirror for students who are familiar with it. Sharing news articles and videos is another way to connect stories to the real world—reading about a current refugee crisis would be a great connection to Alan Gratz's *Refugee* or Andrea Davis Pinkney's *The Red Pencil*.

Connecting the Dots

The books and stories that we share with students will hopefully make a lasting impact on their lives. In turn, we hope that students will leave our schools one day feeling empowered to make a positive difference in the world as they live out their own stories. We will not only inspire students to embrace the American Dream, but also make our country a home where those who seek refuge can truly breathe freely.

My parents'
retirement dinner—
a reminder to all of
us that the journey
is the reward. (Photo
credit: John Vu)

A RETIREMENT
DINNER TOAST

MY PARENTS RETIRED ALMOST AT THE SAME TIME
so we celebrated their milestone with a dinner party at
a Mexican restaurant down the street from their house.
We invited family, friends, and some of their former
coworkers and bosses. I remember the steak fajitas
being really good. We also had wine and beer. It wasn't
a big or fancy party, but it marked an important moment
that had to be memorialized. I wish I could tell you that,
at the perfect point in the celebration, I had gotten up
and tapped my wine glass with my fork to get everyone's

attention to make a toast. I wish I could tell you that in that toast, I was able to communicate everything in my heart about how proud I was of my parents and how grateful I was for their sacrifice and love. But I can't. I'm not sure why, but no one made any speeches that night, and congratulations were shared one-on-one between my parents and the guests. It was a good night, but if I had to do it again, I would have taken a deep breath, stood up, cleared my throat, and asked for everyone's attention.

Although I didn't have much to say that night, luckily in life, there's always a second chance. And now that I've had plenty of time to reflect, I have plenty of things to say. So, if you would indulge me a bit, here's my retirement toast to my parents.

Good evening, everyone. I hope that you are all enjoying the food. It's perfect that we are celebrating the retirement of two Vietnamese Americans at a Mexican restaurant as we sip Italian wine and chug German beer. This is the American Dream. My name is Don Hùng Vu, and I am the eldest child of Hien and Nguyet. On behalf of my family, I'd like to thank you for coming tonight to celebrate a big milestone.

Over three decades ago, my parents left their homeland of Vietnam. They had no choice, as Vietnam was falling to the communist Viet Cong and, as quick as some people decide to go on a beer run to the market, they decided to leave everything they knew behind to save their family. Can you imagine having to do that? Can you imagine having to escape the chaos of war with three children, your mother, and mother-in-law? Can you imagine doing that at the ages where most of us would be in college, worrying about changing our major for the fifth time? I know that it would take all my courage and strength to flee as my parents did and I still wouldn't be so sure that I'd be so successful in the end. But they did it. And they were able to do it with dignity for who they were, faith in God, and love for their family.

Tonight we celebrate the American Dream. It's a beautiful idea—the pursuit of happiness in a country that took in our family at a time when we desperately needed saving. But we know that something that is so precious, this American Dream, comes at a cost. Growing up, my parents were always working, hustling, and trying to balance family life as they were trying to make ends meet. They gave up a lot and sacrificed more than we would ever know. They had to persevere through hard times as they learned a new culture, a new language, and a new way of life. They had to endure prejudice and racism. Some of you may know the story of when my mother started working as a clerk at Safeway and an older woman refused to go into her lane because she "didn't want those people to touch her things." But, when you heard, you came to support her and let her know that she would not stand alone. And my parents never stood alone in their pursuit of the American Dream. The U.S. Marines stood with them when they arrived at the makeshift refugee camp in Camp Pendleton in 1975. The community stood with them when they found a new home and enrolled their kids in school. And businesses stood with them when they took a chance on hiring Vietnamese refugees that could only promise hard work and dedication. A promise that lasted over three decades.

Tonight we celebrate my parents. I'm not going to say that this is the end of a long journey or that they have found at the end of this journey the American Dream. While it has been a long journey for them so far, it is only beginning. And, while we can safely say that they have achieved so much so far, the American Dream isn't something that I would dare say we can achieve in our lifetimes. You see, it's never been about my parents' survival and success. It's always been about their family, their children, their grandchildren. It's about ensuring that their kids are educated and liberated. It's about ensuring that the next generation can live a life that is truly free—to be whomever they want to be in this world. So the pursuit of happiness and the American Dream is never the end but only a beginning.

Please join me in raising a glass to my parents. Bố and Mẹ [Dad and Mom], I look forward to your new beginning and can't wait to hear about your new adventures together. May your pursuit of happiness and the American Dream take you on many journeys to the far corners of the world. And may we never forget the first journey that started it all. We are proud of you and we love you.

10

CELEBRATION

"Celebration happens when the mind unites with the spirit."

—SRI SRI RAVI SHANKAR

How people celebrate and carry out traditions helps define the culture of the community in which they live. Just like Mardi Gras helps define New Orleanian culture, the annual Tết (or the Lunar New Year) festivities help define Vietnamese culture. It's the same for schools. School culture develops and grows through an accumulation of actions, traditions, ceremonies, and celebrations that are aligned to a vision (Fisher, Frey & Pumpian, 2012). As you continue to develop and grow a culture of literacy for all students in your school, you'll find that celebrations and traditions are critical in defining and upholding what is important to you and your community.

Honoring Books and Authors

There are several ways to celebrate literacy by honoring books and authors. Here, I describe a few.

Invite Authors In

What better way to celebrate literacy than to invite your favorite author to campus to talk about his or her latest book? When kids (and adults) meet an author in person, they get an opportunity to ask questions, understand his or her work more deeply, and be inspired. And they might even get a book autographed by the author. For kids steeped in a culture of literacy, that's like a home-run ball signed by your favorite shortstop! Now you may not be able to get Dav Pilkey at your school, but there may be local authors available for class talks, assemblies, and book signings. Consider an author nearby if you don't have funds to pay for transportation or lodging. Some of them will even do a school visit at a reduced cost or for free if you give them the green light to sell their books to kids and families before or after their visit. It's a win-win for all. Authors can make a living and we can buy autographed books to add to our home and school libraries. If an author can't visit your school in person, you may be able to schedule a virtual visit. Since this generation of students is so used to FaceTime, Zoom, and other video platforms, online author visits can be just as inspiring and educational as live ones. In any case, author visits are a great way to engage your students with the people who are writing the books they're reading, and some of those people may inspire your students to write their own books someday.

When choosing authors for visits, keep in mind those who are traditionally underrepresented in the children's book publishing world. Kids need to hear the stories of people from all walks of life—people of color, immigrants, refugees, LGBTQIA people, to name a few. How impactful would it be for a young student from an economically challenged community to meet and listen to an author who grew up in a similar community? How about the impact of a Black author on an auditorium full of middle-class white kids? If you're looking for authors for a school visit, check out groups such as The Society of Children's Book Writers and Illustrators for a general search.

Author and illustrator visits are a fun way to make books come alive for students. Here, our kids loved listening to *The Little Lemon That Leapt*.

Offer Author Residencies

At Barrett Ranch Elementary School, we were lucky enough to be surrounded by many local authors, but we had a special relationship with one author: Les Nuckolls. He's written several fantastic children's books based on events in his life, including *A Boy Named Walter, Growing Up in Africa*, and *Chester the Chimpanzee*. He was orphaned at a young age and then moved from one abusive foster home to another. Through his own determination and grit, as well as with the support of caring teachers, Les created a new life for himself. His stories also include his adventures raising his children (along with Chester the chimpanzee) in Africa for two years.

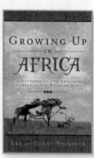

One year, we decided to do something different from the standard author visit from Les. We came up with the idea of having an "author residency." Les spent a few days on campus, met with kids at each grade level, and talked about his books, told stories, and discussed writing and literacy. He also presented at a staff meeting, inspiring teachers with his personal story of struggling in school until the adults took time to help him. Les met with our parents at an evening PTA meeting, and even ate lunch and went to recess with students. One afternoon, he spent a couple of hours talking with students who struggle with behavior about his life and inspired many of them to change their lives in positive ways.

While most author visits are limited to student assemblies, author residencies allow schools to dive deeply into literacy and celebrate it, while building relationships with professional creators of books. They're educational and fun and may inspire your students to tell their own stories.

Recognize Release Dates of New Books

Another way to honor books and authors is to celebrate new books when they are published, beyond very popular books such as the latest installments in the Harry Potter or Dog Man series. After all, a book's release is a big deal!

Sometimes publishers throw parties. Sometimes eager readers wait in line in anticipation for their copies. They look forward to visiting familiar characters in fresh situations and being introduced to new ones.

We don't have to throw a party for the release of every book, but there are other ways to acknowledge the addition of new titles to your school community. Some schools announce them during the morning announcements. Some librarians introduce them every week to students, and reserve a special shelf or table for them. Some librarians go a step further and give birthday parties to new books. If we make new books a big deal in our schools, they become a big deal to our kids.

Don't Forget Student Authors!

A final note on honoring books and authors: Don't forget to include the most important authors at your school—your students! Every day, your students write stories and create amazing characters and illustrations. Every day brings an opportunity to celebrate those stories. When students publish their stories, make sure teachers share them with the school librarian, who should treat them the same way she or he would treat professionally published books—put them on the new-releases shelf, recommend them to others, announce them on the intercom, and so on.

One year, we had students in one class write individual pieces on what they imagined in the "perfect" school, and then compiled those pieces into a book

PURSUIT OF CELEBRATION

Say "Happy Birthday!" to New Books

How do you even find out the release dates of children's books? Well, our good friend John Schu, Ambassador of School Libraries for Scholastic, maintains a public calendar that lists them—every notable book release date (with a description of the book) can be added to your school's calendar. It doesn't get any easier than that! To find his calendar, do an online search for Mr. Schu's blog or go to this link:

http://mrschureads.blogspot.com/2012/01/book-release-calendar.html

and placed it in our school library for other students in other classes to read. We recorded a read-aloud of the book and posted the video on our school YouTube channel. Needless to say, the students were so proud of their work and elated to see it online for the world to enjoy.

Acknowledging Literary Achievements and Accomplishments

When kids work hard to achieve literary goals—whether it's writing a story, participating in a poetry slam, or finishing a 40-book challenge—acknowledge and celebrate those accomplishments. Recognizing literary achievements allows us to celebrate all students, even the student who is new to this country and learning English, or the student who has a learning challenge but has a great story to tell. It's an opportunity for us to engage all kids and let everyone in the community know that they have something worthy to celebrate.

Reinforcing Literacy With School Traditions

Celebrating school traditions is important in sustaining a culture of literacy for all. Many schools already do this unknowingly. Do you have an annual book fair? That is one of those time-honored traditions that kids and families look forward to every year. How about a literacy night when you meet with families and share books and stories?

Think about each tradition at your school and ask yourself if it's worth maintaining. What are the students and their families getting out of it? If you were to cancel it, would they be upset? If you would have a bunch of disappointed kids and parents, then you should probably keep it.

(top) An invitation to the book prom, an idea we borrowed from our friend Todd Nesloney.

(bottom) Myles and Aubrey at the book prom— a celebration where kids bring their favorite books to share with friends and teachers. There's music, dancing, book talking, and even book prom royalty!

Life, Literacy, and the Pursuit of Happiness

Beyond the book fairs and literacy nights, there are other creative literary traditions to consider. The summer after we started our Broncos Read… campaign described in the introduction, my colleagues and I came up with a fun way to continue showing kids that reading is important. I asked teachers and staff members to take photos of themselves reading anywhere, while on vacation. They sent me photos of themselves at the beach, on cruise ships, in medieval castles, at Disneyland, and even in their backyards. I took all of the photos and made them into posters titled "Broncos Read…". At the beginning of the school year, we hung the posters throughout the school, and the kids loved looking at them to find out where the adults in the building had been during summer break and what they read.

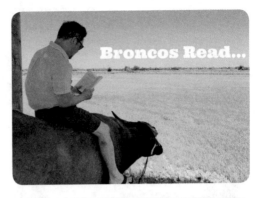

Broncos Read… posters remind everyone that reading can happen anywhere and anytime.

The poster initiative became an annual tradition. Each summer, the teachers and staff members would try to make their photos as creative and wild as ever. One year, we had teachers reading books while riding a roller coaster at Disneyland. You know those photos they take of you during the ride and then try to sell you after the ride? The ones where your faces are all contorted and you're screaming in horror? Well, the teachers planned it so that, right before a terrifying moment on the ride, they all pulled out their books and pretended to read.

When I went back to Vietnam one summer, I met a rice farmer outside the small town of Hoi An and asked him if I could take a photo of myself reading on his water buffalo. He looked at me funny, chuckled, and let me hop on for my Broncos Read… photo. This tradition became so popular that kids and families started taking photos of themselves reading during vacation!

Some schools celebrate literacy in equally creative ways throughout the school year. For example, Parma Elementary School in Michigan has a tradition of sending a children's book as a gift to families whenever a new child is born. It's a small gesture but a meaningful one that signals what is truly valued in the school community—family and literacy.

What literary traditions do you currently celebrate? Can you think of new ones that would pull in every member of your school community? This is the fun stuff. There are so many ways to celebrate literacy, and so many ways to turn those celebrations into traditions that help create a culture of literacy.

PURSUIT OF CELEBRATION

Recognize Traditions to Build Cultural Understanding

Do you know the cultural traditions that are important to your immigrant and refugee students and their families? They usually involve food and fun, and recognizing them at school can be an easy way to make those students and families feel welcome and included. By no means is this a comprehensive culturally responsive solution to inequity in schools, but it opens a window to your students' and families' lived experiences. It is a good place to begin. When I was a teacher in Oakland, many of my students were Vietnamese immigrants, and I knew that every fall, they were celebrating Tết Trung Thu, or the Mid-Autumn Festival, at home with their families. So I decided that the entire class would celebrate the festival by sharing books and legends about the holiday. My students and I would also spend time sampling traditional mooncakes and making paper lanterns for a parade. Many of the Vietnamese families were happy to help and felt pride in sharing their culture. And many of the other families were just as happy to have their children learn about a new culture and different way of life. How can you celebrate Día de los Muertos to honor a tradition of your Mexican American students and their families? How can you recognize Eid for those immigrants and refugees from Syria or other Muslim-dominant countries? There are many children's books on traditions from around the world. By sharing them with your students, you build a culture of understanding and acceptance that is fun and meaningful.

Life, Literacy, and the Pursuit of Happiness

Making Literacy Extraordinary

Sometimes magic happens. It happened to my colleagues and me a few years ago when we were talking about using our pod rooms for something besides storage. On our campus, every three classrooms were connected by a pod room—a space intended for pullout small-group work. We had 24 classrooms, so there were eight pods. As I was walking through the building one day after school, complaining about how the pod rooms had been repurposed into disorganized storage areas, second-grade teacher Kendra Barrett came up with the idea to make them reading lounges that would house shared libraries among the three classrooms. Each lounge would have comfortable furniture, and its design would be inspired by a favorite book. Creating these lounges would support our goal of increasing independent reading time for kids as well as the number of books available to teachers and students. I loved the idea! It was strongly tied to our vision of reading in our school, and it enabled us to finally get rid of some of the junk that had been collecting dust for so long!

I called up our local Ikea store and asked the manager if she wanted to collaborate on our reading lounge project. I enticed her by explaining that we'd have a local news channel broadcast the "unveiling" of these lounges, and Ikea would be a big part of that report. (In truth, I had no idea how I'd pull that off, but kept the faith!) The manager got back to me a few days later to tell me that she would provide furniture for two of the lounges and lend us her showroom designer to help with the plans!

I also reached out to our local Orchard Supply Hardware store, and the manager there, who was a parent in the school, agreed to provide paint and other supplies. We were good to go—at least for the first two reading lounges!

Our teachers were excited. They came in on weekends to clean, paint, and assemble furniture. When the first reading lounge was revealed to the staff—the Hatchet Reading Lounge (inspired by Gary Paulsen's book)— made to look like a forest with debris from a plane crash, everyone was hooked. It was

The Journey Trilogy reading lounge is based on Aaron Becker's magical picture books. Parent Jack Austin spent over a week painting the mural.

Readers are transported to a farm house and barn in our Charlotte's Web reading lounge.

not a matter of if we could create all eight lounges, but how quickly we could.

Over the next year and a half, we secured thousands of dollars through local grants and donations. We partnered with Scholastic to get thousands of books into the reading lounges and eventually had eight reading lounges for our students to fully immerse themselves while reading in school. In addition to Hatchet, we created reading lounges with these themes: The Journey Trilogy (Aaron Becker), Island of the Blue Dolphins, Where the Wild Things Are, Charlotte's Web, Mercy Watson, Dr. Seuss, and The Jungle Book.

It was a magical project that started with one person who had a good idea and was fueled by the passion and creativity of everyone else. While you may not have the budget or wherewithal to create reading lounges at your school, there is magic hiding somewhere. If you have a vision and a culture to support it, anything is possible.

And when magic happens, celebrate it. Share it joyously with one another. The time you, your colleagues, students, and families have together is not everlasting. Students and families come to us and eventually move on. Our colleagues sometimes leave us. You may eventually find yourself on another path.

I knew that when I decided to leave Barrett Ranch, I would miss it with all my heart. In my time as principal there, I struggled and triumphed with my colleagues. We had created a community of learners and readers who cared for one another. We had created a magical place for our students, our families, and ourselves. We will remember the traditions, celebrations, and ceremonies because they helped us create our culture of literacy for all. And if we are serious about creating a culture of literacy for all, we must be open to inviting and creating magic in our schools.

Life, Literacy, and the Pursuit of Happiness

Malala inspired the world. And her life inspired our school to make a difference.

ONE CHILD, ONE TEACHER

AT BARRETT RANCH ELEMENTARY SCHOOL, OUR THEME for one year was "One child, one teacher, one book, and one pen can change the world." It's a quote from the youngest-ever Nobel Peace Prize winner, Malala Yousafzai. Because those words were so meaningful to us, and spoke to our beliefs and vision of education as a staff, we put them everywhere. We believed that every child had the potential to make a positive difference in the world—and every teacher had a pivotal role to play in helping to guide and support each child. And we believed that literacy—from reading the stories of others to writing our own stories to be shared with the world—was the vehicle for change. "One child, one teacher, one book, and one pen can change the world." We made sure everyone knew the story of the Pakistani girl who believed so much in the power of literacy and education, she risked everything she had to preserve it.

Malala Yousafzai was born in the beautiful Swat Valley of Pakistan. When she was still in school, the Taliban's takeover of parts of Pakistan reached her home. Once in power, the extremist militants banned from their new society many activities they believed were against Sharia law, such as music, movies, and dancing. The Taliban also banned girls from attending school. In 2008 alone, they had destroyed (as in physically bombing them) over 150 schools. Malala spoke out against the Taliban and even wrote an anonymous blog for the BBC, detailing life under Taliban rule. Speaking out for the education of all girls, she became a target of the extremists. On October 9, 2012, a gunman boarded a school bus and shot 15-year-old Malala in the left side of her head as she was heading home from class.

If the story ended there, it would be tragic, but we would still be inspired by the courage and strength of one young girl. As destiny would have it, though, Malala survived the attempt on her life, was airlifted to England with her family for emergency surgery, and recovered. She and her family could not return to their homeland for obvious safety concerns. They had become refugees.

Soon afterward, from her newly adopted home in the United Kingdom, Malala began her tireless advocacy for girls. Her work in fighting for the literacy and educational rights of all girls—through the Malala Fund—earned her the Nobel Peace Prize at the young age of 17. In 2020, the refugee from Pakistan graduated from Oxford University with a degree in Philosophy, Politics, and Economics. She continues to work for the education of all girls everywhere and is living proof that one child, one teacher, one book, and one pen can indeed change the world.

As teachers, we don't often witness the impact our students have on the world. Did we make a difference? For Malala Yousafzai, the teacher that inspired her was her own father, Ziauddin Yousafzai, schoolteacher, head of school, and educational activist. He believed that a girl's worth equaled a boy's, and that his daughter should have the same opportunities as his sons. As the Taliban was rising in power, he encouraged his daughter to fight for her rights, to speak up in the face of extremism, and to advocate for others. It was dangerous for her and the family, but it would have been more dangerous if they had remained silent. Malala says of her father, "He gave me wings." And he is now proud to say that he is the "youngest-ever father of a Nobel Prize winner."

Educators give students wings to fly free every day. We do that the same way Ziauddin gave Malala wings—by encouraging our students to be true to themselves, helping them find their voices, and guiding them to be a voice of righteousness for others. During the year we celebrated Malala's story, we did a whole-school book study on her autobiography for children, *Malala's Magic Pencil*. (Yes, she has done it all: Oxford, Nobel Peace Prize, inspiration to millions, and a children's book author!) We wanted all of our kids to know Malala's story. We wanted them to see a young person use her education to make a difference in the world. We wanted our kids to see a woman of color—someone who had faced nearly insurmountable challenges—find the strength to change the world for the better. We wanted our students to see themselves in her story.

One afternoon, as I was reading *Malala's Magic Pencil* to a group of second-grade students in one of our reading lounges, I looked down at one student as she gently stroked her hijab while listening intently. I gave her an encouraging look as I stopped to turn the page.

She took the cue and said, loud enough for the whole group to hear, "I'm wearing what she wears."

I looked at her with a smile and said, "It's a beautiful hijab that you have on. How does it make you feel that Malala wears hijabs, too?"

Without hesitation, she said, "It makes me happy. It makes me proud." And, in that instance, I was reminded that one book can change the world. It definitely changed the world of that one child. And, as we all hope and believe, that one child will someday make a positive difference in the world because her teacher believed in her potential to do so.

11

AND NOW, COMPASSION

"For to be free is not merely to cast off one's chains, but to live in a way that respects and enhances the freedom of others."

—NELSON MANDELA

A few summers ago, I had the incredible opportunity to travel back to Vietnam for the summer with my wife, Maria, and daughter, Cate. I had not been back there since a post-college backpacking trip with a friend. Maria and Cate had never been. Our vacation plans had serendipitously coincided with my parents', as they were ending their trip through parts of Asia with their retired friends.

During the first few days of our vacation and the last leg of my parents' trip, we spent several days all together in the bustling city where it all began. Saigon, renamed Ho Chi Minh City to honor the communist leader who led the Viet Cong to victory over the Americans, is an enormous city of contradictions, with over nine million people. It's a city of street food vendors hawking noodles in front of Gucci and Prada storefronts. It's a city of cyclo (a bike-pedaled carriage) drivers riding next to a family of four on a small scooter, zipping by a candy-red Lamborghini sports car. It's a city that contains constant reminders of its colonial past, but one populated with a young majority of citizens who weren't even born until after the war. It's a new city, an old city. It's a city full of hustle and bustle, as entrepreneurs try to make a bundle (or at least a living), while a communist government that went to war to rid the country of American capitalistic values realizes that these same ideals are pushing Vietnam toward becoming a regional force in Southeast Asia.

We spent the first two days visiting the church where my parents were married (and I was baptized) and their old neighborhood, and chatting with long-lost friends and family members who were left behind. On our third day together, my parents asked us if we wanted to travel about three hours out of the city to tour the Mekong Delta. We would visit some of the famous floating markets, visit some farms, and tour a homestead to catch a glimpse of rural life in Vietnam. Of course, we said yes.

Forty-three years later. Back where it all started, with my parents, along with my wife, Maria, and daughter Cate—Saigon, Vietnam, 2018.

On the way to the Mekong Delta, we picked up one of my mom's friends whom she hadn't seen since they were little girls in elementary school. It was a sweet sight—two women in their mid-60s holding hands as they walked along a fish farm levee, reminiscing about the past and talking about how widely their paths had diverged after the American War. (What else would they call the war in Vietnam?)

My mother's friend was accompanied by her nephew, a young man in his early 20s, who had just graduated from college with a degree in architecture. He was quiet, respectful, thin, and clean-shaven, and he looked younger than his age. I asked him about his career plans and he reluctantly said that he wasn't quite sure. He said that he was lucky enough to get into college— he had great grades and high test scores, and earned a scholarship to pay for tuition—but he didn't have the connections or money to land him a job.

In Vietnam, good-paying government or private-sector jobs are hard to come by. Getting one requires personal connections and, in many cases, bribery. This is an issue of power and class, usually leaving the poor without many options, no matter how talented or educated they are. This was the first time on the trip I was told about the struggles of people like that man, but it wasn't the last. Over the following weeks, we met many young Vietnamese as we traveled the country. Many of them had similar stories. For example, we met taxi drivers who were college graduates but couldn't find jobs in their chosen fields. We also met drivers who didn't even apply to college because they figured they would end up driving taxis anyway. Why go to college, waste valuable money, lose valuable time, only to find yourself at a dead end? Because only the well-connected or wealthy receive many of society's benefits in Vietnam, many of its young people forgo college and enter the service industry or start their own businesses. It is a corrupt system that protects those with money and power. And the government can be just as corrupt. Getting government jobs requires the same privileges—connections and wealth—and those without them too often never find employment.

Given what I've said thus far, it may be surprising to hear that Vietnam is one of the most literate countries in the world. According to the World Bank, the literacy rate in 2018 for Vietnamese over the age of 15 is 95 percent (2020). While government programs and initiatives have stressed the value of literacy, they fall short in providing the opportunities for Vietnamese citizens to use their reading and writing skills to improve their lives and promote the development and advancement of the country.

On my journey that summer, I realized that you can have literacy, but you also need to have hope—hope for a brighter future in a system that will allow you to attain your dreams of success.

On my journey that summer, I realized that you can have literacy, but you also need to have hope—hope for a brighter future in a system that will allow you to attain your dreams of success. There's a saying that if you think you can catch the bus that's departed, you'll run for it. And the opposite is true. If you don't think you will catch that bus, you won't waste your time running for it. And I believe that is an apt metaphor for many young people in Vietnam, who had little hope that their education would help them improve their lives. I also believe that is the case for many young people in America. Do all of our students believe they can catch the bus if they run for it?

Our students need to hope for something real when they finish their journey through our schools. If we envision literacy as freedom, then hope for a better tomorrow is what fuels that vision. If those in power, those running our society's systems (including us educators), don't see that there can't be freedom without hope, then we will have missed the point.

As I write, I realize we are on a precarious part of the path. We are in the middle of a pandemic that is holding us hostage in our homes and schools as we quarantine. We are witnesses to horrible injustices against our Black brothers and sisters, and a new movement in support of Black lives has pushed our society to question itself and its history. There is more prejudice and intolerance, as evidenced by the rising number of hate crimes against people who are traditionally marginalized—people who are not white, not straight, not Christian. As a nation, moderation of political and social thought is becoming rare, as we push one another into partisan extremes.

If those in power, those running our society's systems (including us educators), don't see that there can't be freedom without hope, then we will have missed the point.

This is the path in America that we find ourselves on now. And as we travel that path, we can see the disparities of people who live the American Dream and people who don't. Not unlike those young people in Vietnam, some of our students and their families have watched the bus come and go—and feel they're not going to catch it, no matter how quickly they run.

Compassion: The Seventh Condition

Because of everything we've experienced since the beginning of 2020, building a culture of literacy will not mean much if we don't allow compassion for others—the immigrants, the refugees, the majority and the minority, the rich and the poor, the Black and the white—to flow into every aspect of our work. Without compassion, we cannot provide hope for a brighter future. Without compassion, we cannot work to change the system so that the bus leaves no American behind. Without compassion for our students and their families who struggle every day, we lose sight of our calling. At the intersection of compassion and the other six conditions, we see how literacy can help us all realize the promise of America.

Compassion in Commitment

When we are committed to improving ourselves, our colleagues, and our schools, we must acknowledge that real progress occurs when we grow from our shortcomings. Mistakes and failures are part of the process. Compassion allows us to forgive ourselves when we stumble. For others on their journey—whether they're expanding their social circle, questioning their thoughts about race, or making their hiring practices more inclusive—our compassion lets them know that we support their efforts and commend their progress. As we work for equity in our schools, compassion will not only remind us of our responsibilities to all students and families, but will also propel us to move forward boldly.

Compassion in Clock and Collection

When students are away from school for long periods of time, we must think of ways to combat the possible academic slide, especially for our students from under-resourced communities. Those students may not have had as much time reading independently at home for various reasons—including access to books, or lack thereof. If families have limited home libraries, limited access to the Internet, limited access to community libraries and bookstores, and/or limited funds to purchase books, their children will have limited opportunities to read independently at home. Compassion allows us to see that what separates those students from others are money and resources. We must work harder to bring books and other reading materials into their homes. Compassion for others allows us to understand this disgraceful disparity and pushes us to do everything in our power to even the playing field.

Compassion in Conversation

For many of our immigrant and refugee students, having literate conversations in English at home may be difficult because their parents are not fluent in English. Another obstacle to literate conversations, for those students as well for students from lower socioeconomic backgrounds, is time: Parents may not be available to read and talk about reading because they're working overtime or juggling multiple jobs to make ends meet. Therefore, many students lose out on building their literacy skills through conversation. Compassion allows us to think about how we can help those students, how we can find extra

Life, Literacy, and the Pursuit of Happiness

time for literate conversations at school and creative ways to promote them at home. It allows us to reflect on the struggles that those families may face every day and gives us some insight into how to support them through our work.

Compassion in Connection and Celebration

How traumatic must it be to live in a society that tells you that you are not worthy? A society in which everyone does not agree that Black and Brown lives matter? A society in which it's okay to tell some citizens to go back to where they came from? Even the daily microaggressions that our immigrants, refugees, and other marginalized people experience add up, and the wounds fester. These people come to our schools every day, carrying that trauma with them. As compassionate educators, we understand the power of literacy to help our immigrant and refugee students. And as such, we fight to ensure that all kids see themselves in stories and see their worth in the world. When we gather to celebrate traditions and share everyone's stories, when we express compassion, we redefine what America is and what stories will continue to resonate.

We Are Making the Path

Building and sustaining a culture of literacy for all is not an easy task. I am asked quite often by educators how long it took for us at Barrett Ranch to build one. My answer is always the same. You start when you take that first action step toward the vision, but the work is never finished. It should never be finished. Think of it as a journey, not a destination. Along the path, you will make mistakes and fail. But you will keep going, bolstered by what you believe is good for all kids. And, conversely, you will find success and move further along your path. As Paulo Freire suggests, you will make the path by walking.

Building a culture of literacy in schools for all is more important now than ever, given the inequities in our society, as well as in our school communities. If there is a place where the path can be made for a better America, it's in our schools. It's probably the only place, actually. With compassion and through hope, creating the conditions of culture in schools will help us make a positive difference in the lives of all students. It can change the world. One child, one teacher, one book, and one pen at a time.

DR. VU'S HOT READS!

Immigrant and Refugee Stories

Alma and How She Got Her Name by Juana Martinez-Neal (2018). Candlewick Press.

The Arabic Quilt: An Immigrant Story by Aya Khalil (2020). Tilbury House Publishers.

The Best We Could Do: An Illustrated Memoir by Thi Bui (2017). Abrams Books.

Blue Sky White Stars by Sarvinder Naberhaus (2017). Dial Books.

City of Thorns: Nine Lives in the World's Largest Refugee Camp by Ben Rawlence (2016). Picador Publishing.

The Crossing: My Journey to the Shattered Heart of Syria by Samar Yazbek (2016). Ebury Press.

Dear Primo: A Letter to My Cousin by Duncan Tonatiuh. (2010). Abrams Books.

A Different Pond by Bao Phi (2017). Capstone Young Readers.

The Displaced: Refugee Writers on Refugee Lives edited by Viet Thanh Nguyen (2019). Abrams Books.

The Distance Between Us: Young Readers Edition by Reyna Grande (2016). Aladdin Books.

Dreamers by Yuyi Morales (2018). Neal Porter Books.

Esperanza Rising by Pam Muñoz Ryan (2000). Scholastic.

The Far Away Brothers: Two Young Migrants and the Making of an American Life by Lauren Markham (2018). Crown Books.

Front Desk by Kelly Yang (2019). Scholastic.

The Hundred-Year Walk: An Armenian Odyssey by Dawn Anahid MacKeen (2017). Mariner Books.

I'm an Immigrant Too! by Mem Fox (2018). Beach Lane Books.

Imagine by Juan Felipe Herrera (2018). Candlewick Press.

Inside Out & Back Again by Thanhha Lai (2013). HarperCollins Publishers.

A Long Petal of the Sea: A Novel by Isabel Allende (2020). Ballantine Books.

Lubna and Pebble by Wendy Meddour (2019). Dial Books.

Malala's Magic Pencil by Malala Yousafzai (2017). Little, Brown Books for Young Readers.

The Name Jar by Yangsook Choi (2003). Dragonfly Books.

Other Words for Home by Jasmine Warga (2019). Balzer & Bray/Harperteen Books.

Refugee by Alan Gratz (2017). Scholastic.

The Refugees by Viet Thanh Nguyen (2018). Grove Press.

The Ungrateful Refugee: What Immigrants Never Tell You by Dina Nayeri (2020). Catapult Books.

Voices on the Move: An Anthology By and About Refugees edited by Domnica Radulescu and Roxana Cazan (2020). Solis Press.

We Are Displaced: My Journey and Stories from Refugee Girls Around the World by Malala Yousafzai (2019). Little, Brown Books for Young Readers.

Yo-Yo & Yeou-Cheng Ma: Finding Their Way by Ai-Ling Louie (2012). Dragoneagle Press.

Other Children's Books Cited

All American Boys by Jason Reynolds and Brendan Kiely (2017). Atheneum/Caitlyn Dlouhy Books.

The Book With No Pictures by B. J. Novak (2014). Dial Books.

A Boy Named Walter by Les and Genny Nuckolls (2011). Cedar Fort Publishing.

Chester the Chimpanzee by Les and Genny Nuckolls (2012). Sweetwater Books.

Growing Up in Africa by Les and Genny Nuckolls (2007). Cedar Fort Publishing.

The Hate U Give by Angie Thomas (2017). Balzer & Bray/Harperteen Books.

Last Stop on Market Street by Matt de la Peña (2015). G.P. Putnam's Sons Books for Young Readers.

The Little Lemon That Leapt by Karen Sanders-Betts (2015). Little Lemon Production House.

Wonder by R.J. Palacio (2012). Knopf Books for Young Readers.

For updates, go to scholastic.com/LifeLiteracyResources.

REFERENCES

Ahmed, S. (2018). *Being the change: Lessons and strategies to teach social comprehension*. Portsmouth, NH: Heinemann.

Allington, R. (2002). What I've learned about effective reading instruction from a decade of studying exemplary elementary classroom teachers. *Phi Delta Kappan, 83*(10), 740–747.

Allington, R. (2012). *What really matters for struggling readers: Designing research-based programs*. Boston, MA: Pearson.

Allington, R., & Gabriel, R. (2012, March). Every child, every day. *Educational Leadership, 69*(6), 10–15.

Allington, R., & McGill-Franzen, A. (2013). *Summer reading: Closing the rich/poor reading achievement gap*. New York: Teachers College Press.

American Academy of Pediatrics. (2014). Policy Statement.

Anderson, R. C., Wilson, P. T., Fielding, L. G. (1988). Growth in reading and how children spend their time outside of school. *Reading Research Quarterly, 23*(3), 285–303.

Applebee, A., Langer, J., Nystrand, M., & Gamoran, A. (2003). Discussion-based approaches to developing understanding: Classroom instruction and student performance in middle and high school English. *American Educational Research Journal, 40*(2), 685–730.

Bambrick-Santoyo, P., Settles, A., & Worrell, J. (2013). *Great habits, great readers*. Hoboken, NJ: Wiley.

Bernstein, H. (2010). "The importance of reading to your child." *A Parent's Life*. Cambridge, MA: Harvard School of Medicine.

Bishop, R. S. (1990). Mirrors, windows, and sliding glass doors. *Perspectives, 1*(3), ix–xi.

Boushey, G., & Moser, J. (2014). *The Daily 5: Fostering literacy independence in the elementary grades*. Portland, ME: Stenhouse.

Breiseth, L., Robertson, K., & Lafond, S. (2011). *A guide for engaging ELL families: Twenty strategies for school leaders*. Retrieved from Colorín Colorado website: http://www.colorincolorado.org/sites/default/files/Engaging_ELL_Families_FINAL.pdf.

Castellón, M., Cheuk, T., Greene, R., Mercado-Garcia, D., Santos, M., Skarin, R., & Zerkel, L. (2015). *Schools to learn from: How six high schools graduate English language learners college and career ready*. Stanford, CA: Stanford University, Stanford Graduate School of Education. Retrieved from http://ell.stanford.edu/sites/default/files/Schools%20to%20Learn%20From%20.pdf.

Calkins, L. (2015). *Units of study for teaching reading: A workshop curriculum, Grades K–5*. Portsmouth, NH: Heinemann.

Calkins, L., Ehrenworth, M., & Topping, K. (2012). *Pathways to the Common Core: Accelerating achievement*. New York: Scholastic.

Cooper, H., Charlton, K., Valentine, J. C., & Muhlenbruck, L. (2000). Making the most of summer school: A meta-analytic and narrative review. *Monographs of the Society for Research in Child Development, 65*(1), 1–118.

Cooperative Children's Book Center School of Education, University of Wisconsin-Madison. (2020, October 27). Data on books by and about Black, Indigenous and People of Color published for children and teens. Retrieved October 30, 2020, from https://ccbc.education.wisc.edu/literature-resources/ccbc-diversity-statistics/books-by-and-or-about-poc-2018/.

Cunningham, A., & Stanovich, K. (1998). What reading does for the mind. *American Educator, 22*(1-2), 8–15.

Cunningham, A., & Zibulsky, J. (2014). *Book smart: How to develop and support successful, motivated readers*. New York: Oxford University Press.

Dean, C. B., & Marzano, R. J. (2013). *Classroom instruction that works: Research-based strategies for increasing student achievement*. Boston, MA: Pearson Education.

Espinosa, C., & Ascenzi-Moreno, L. (2021). *Rooted in strength: Using translanguaging to grow multilingual readers and writers*. New York: Scholastic.

Evans, M., Kelley, J., Sikora, J., & Treiman, D. (2010). Family scholarly culture and educational success: Books and schooling in 27 nations. *Research in Social Stratification and Mobility, 28*(2), 171–197.

Everett, C. (2017, July 15). Truth or dare? NerdTalk 2017. ImagineLit. http://www.imaginelit.com/news/2017/7/12/nerdtalk2017.

Fisher, D., Frey, N., & Pumpian, I. (2012). *How to create a culture of achievement in your school and classroom*. Alexandria, VA: ASCD.

Fountas, I., & Pinnell, G. (2012). *Comprehension clubs*. New York: Scholastic.

Gallagher, K. (2009). *Readacide*. Portland, ME: Stenhouse.

Goldenberg, C. (2011). Reading instruction for English language learners. In M. Kamil, P. D. Pearson, E. Moje, & P. Afflerbach (Eds.). *Handbook of Reading Research*, Vol. IV. Newark, DE: International Reading Association.

Guthrie, J. (2004). Teaching for literacy engagement. *Journal of Literacy Research, 36*(1), 1–28.

Guthrie, J., & Humenick, N. (2004). Motivating students to read: Evidence of classroom practices that increase motivation and achievement. In P. McCardle & V. Chhabra (Eds.), *The Voice of Evidence in Reading Research*. Baltimore, MD: Paul H. Brookes.

Guthrie, J., Wigfield, A., & Klauda, S. (2012). Adolescents' engaging in academic literacy. Retrieved from http://www.cori.umd.edu/research-publications/2012_adolescents_engagement_ebook.pdf.

Hiebert, F., & Reutzel, R. (2010). *Revisiting silent reading: New directions for teachers and researchers*. Newark, DE: International Reading Association.

Kids & Family Reading Report: 7th Edition. (2019). Conducted by YouGov and Scholastic. Retrieved from https://www.scholastic.com/readingreport/home.html.

Kim, J. (2009). Summer reading and summer not: Fighting the summer reading slump. Retrieved from http://www.uknow.gse.harvard.edu/teaching/TC321.html.

Layne, S. L. (2012). *Igniting a passion for reading: Successful strategies for building lifetime readers*. New York: Scholastic.

Mapp, K. L., Carver, I., & Lander, J. (2019). *Powerful partnerships: A teacher's guide to engaging families for student success*. New York: Scholastic.

Marzano, R. (2004). *Building background knowledge for academic achievement: Research on what works in schools*. Alexandria, VA: ASCD.

Marzano, R., Pickering, D., & Pollock, J. (2013). *Classroom instruction that works: Research-based strategies for increasing student achievement*. Alexandria, VA: ASCD.

McGill-Franzen, A., Ward, N., & Cahill, M. (2016). Summers: Some are reading, some are not! It matters. *The Reading Teacher, 69*(6), 585–596.

McQuillan, J. (1998). *The literacy crisis: False claims and real solutions*. Portsmouth, NH: Heinemann.

Miller, D. (2009). *The book whisperer: Awakening the inner reader in every child*. San Francisco, CA: Jossey-Bass.

Mol, S. E., & Bus, A. G. (2011). To read or not to read: A meta-analysis of print exposure from infancy to early adulthood. *Psychological Bulletin, 137*, 267–296.

Muhammad, G. (2020). *Cultivating genius: An equity framework for culturally and historically responsive literacy*. New York: Scholastic.

Mullis, I., & Martin, M. (2007). *Overview of PIRLS 2006 results* [news release]. Boston: International Association for the Evaluation of Educational Achievement and TIMSS & Progress in International Reading Literacy (PIRLS) International Study Center.

National Assessment of Educational Progress. (2005). *The nation's report card: Reading 2005*. Washington, D.C.: Perie, M., Grigg, W., & Donahue, L.

NCTE. (2019, November 7). Statement on independent reading. Retrieved December 14, 2020, from https://ncte.org/statement/independent-reading/.

Needlman, R. (2014). "How a Doctor Discovered Reading." In L. Bridges (Ed.), *Open a world of possible: Real stories about the joy and power of reading*. New York: Scholastic.

Neuman, S., & Celano, D. (2001). Access to print in low- and middle- and low-middle-income communities: An ecological study of four neighborhoods. *Reading Research Quarterly, 36*(1), 8–26.

Neuman, S., & Celano, D. (2012). Worlds apart: One city, two libraries and ten years of watching inequality grow. *American Educator, 36*(3), 13–23.

Nystrand, M. (2006). Research on the role of classroom discourse as it affects reading comprehension. *Research in the Teaching of English, 40*(4), 392–412.

Pink, D. (2011). *Drive: The surprising truth about what motivates us*. New York: Riverhead Books.

Pruzinsky, T. (2014, March). Read books. Every day. Mostly for pleasure. *English Journal, 103*(4), 25–30.

Reynolds, J. (2017, October 24). *CBS This Morning*. https://www.youtube.com/watch?v=lC6W88wgYDY

Routman, R. (2014). *Read, write, lead: Breakthrough strategies for schoolwide literacy success*. Alexandria, VA: ACSD.

Senge, P. M. (2006). *The fifth discipline*. London, England: Random House Business.

Sewell, E. (2003). Students' choice of books during self-selected reading. EDRS opinion papers.

Shah, N. (2012). Educating immigrant students a challenge in the U.S., elsewhere. *Education Week, 31*(16), 24–28.

Shanahan, T. (2012, March 20). Part 2: Practical guidance on pre-reading lessons. Retrieved from https://shanahanonliteracy.com/blog/part-2-practical-guidance-on-pre-reading-lessons.

Sinek, S., Mead, D., & Docker, P. (2017). *Find your why: A practical guide for discovering purpose for you and your team*. New York: Portfolio/Penguin.

Stern, L. (1981). Response to Vietnamese refugees: Surveys of public opinion. *Social Work, 26*(4), 306–311. Retrieved November 9, 2019, from http://www.jstor.org/stable/23713333.

Storer, C. (2017). *Homecoming King* [Film]. Art and Industry.

Swan, E., Coddington, C., & Guthrie, J. (2010). Engaged silent reading: Revisiting silent reading. In E. Hiebert & R. Reutzel (Eds.), *Revisiting silent reading: New directions for teachers and researchers*. Newark, DE: International Reading Association.

Teacher & Principal School Report: Focus on Literacy. (2017). Conducted by YouGov and Scholastic. Retrieved from https://www.scholastic.com/content/dam/tpr-downloads/Scholastic-Teacher-and-Principal-School-Report-Literacy.pdf.

Trelease, J. (2006). *The read-aloud handbook*. London, England: Penguin Books.

Umansky, I., & Dumont, H. (2019). English learner labeling: How English learner status shapes teacher perceptions of student skills & the moderating role of bilingual instructional settings. (EdWorkingPaper: 19–94). Retrieved from Annenberg Institute at Brown University: http://www.edworkingpapers.com/ai19-94.

UNICEF Office of Research (2017). Building the future: Children and the sustainable development goals in rich countries. *Innocenti Report Card 14*, UNICEF Office of Research – Innocenti, Florence.

U.S. Department of Agriculture, National School Lunch Program Fact Sheet (2017). Retrieved October 1, 2020, from https://fns-prod.azureedge.net/sites/default/files/resource-files/NSLPFactSheet.pdf.

U.S. Department of Education, National Center for Education Statistics, National Teacher and Principal Survey (2020). Public school teacher data file, 2017-2018. Retrieved October 1, 2020, from https://nces.ed.gov/datapoints/2020103.asp.

U.S. Department of State, Refugee Processing Center (2020). Refugee Admissions Reports. Retrieved from https://www.wrapsnet.org/admissions-and-arrivals/.

World Bank (2020). Literacy Rate, Adult Total (% of People Ages 15 and Above)-Vietnam. Retrieved from https://data.worldbank.org/indicator/SE.ADT.LITR.ZS?locations=VN.

INDEX